Sugar and spice?
Bullying in single-sex schools

Celestine Keise

First published in 1992 by Trentham Books Limited

Trentham Books Limited
Westview House
734 London Road
Oakhill
Stoke-on-Trent
Staffordshire
England ST4 5NP

British Library Cataloguing Publication Data
British Cataloguing Publication Data are available from British Library

ISBN: 0 948080 72 8

Designed and typeset by Trentham Print Design, Chester
and printed by Bemrose Shafron Limited, Chester.

Contents

Introduction

A major aim of this study was to reveal how bullying is conceptualised and defined by girls and boys, and to identify the similarities and differences in the bullying behaviour of boys and girls and the lessons that can be learnt from this for schools and LEAs wishing to address the problem. What became very apparent, very quickly, from my work in the two schools is that bullying is not the prerogative of just one sex or 'race' or class. Both schools were experiencing it and both were unsure about how to deal with it.

My particular interest, as a General Inspector with responsibility for sex equality, is in the management of change and how my research can influence policy development within the LEA. I am still acting in a supporting role to schools, and in particular to two of the original schools I worked with as gender advisory teacher. I continue to advise and provide school-based as well as borough wide INSET on how to develop a whole school approach to dealing with harassment and bullying.

When I started the research as an advisory teacher, the focus was on racial and sexual harassment. Some schools felt, however, that whereas these may or may not have been issues for them as a whole school, bullying (seen as a form of harassment) was a common experience for all school students and one with which they were more immediately concerned. Although I have worked with a number of different schools, for the purposes of this study I shall focus mainly on work with two single sex comprehensive schools — one an all-girls school and the other an all-boys school, referred to respectively as Lamont Girls' School and Bankside Boys' School.

For the purposes of the study, I used the definitions of bullying identified by the Burnage Report and in the ILEA's response to the Report, and also as characterised by Valerie Besag. She proposes that there are four facets to the problem of bullying:

1. It may be verbal, physical or psychological in nature.

2. It may be in the form of a socially acceptable behaviour, as in a highly competitive approach to academic, sporting or social success, which, by intent, makes others feel inferior or causes distress.

3. It is necessarily a repetitive attack which causes distress not only at the time of each attack, but also by the threat of future attacks.

4. It is characterised by the dominance of the powerful over the powerless in whatever context.

    In summary, bullying is a behaviour which can be defined as the repeated attack — physical, psychological, social or verbal — by those in a position of power, on those who are powerless to resist, with the intention of causing distress for their own gain or gratification.

Central to the study is the need to make explicit the damaging effect of bullying on victims, bullies, bystanders, the wider school community and the school ethos. Such negative behaviour frequently hinders learning. The resultant continuum of absenteeism, truancy, illness, loss of confidence and self-esteem, suicide and murder, that can be the end result for the victim, has serious and obvious consequences for the victim's ability to learn and to achieve, for the bully's future social development and for the whole school environment.

Acknowledgements

I wish to thank the staff and students of Lamont Girls' School and Bankside Boys' School, Frances Magee (former ILEA Inspector for Equal Opportunities Gender) and Chris Webb, Director of Education, without whom this study would not have been possible. Thanks also to friends, family and colleagues for their support, advice, and encouragement and, in particular, to Ran Mangat who helped me to make sense of the word processor and to Gaby Weiner, my tutor.

Chapter 1
Literature review

In an earlier project for the Open University MA in Education, E813 Gender and Education, I explored the effects of sexual harassment on the learning and achievement of a small group of first year girls in a co-educational secondary school. I suggested possible strategies that schools could adopt (a) to raise awareness of the issue and (b) to bring about change (Open University — *Reluctant Masters* 1989). I also considered the single-sex versus mixed school debate and explored the concept of masculinity for male students. One serious limitation of E813 was the insufficient focus on the links between gender, race and class and a recognition of this deficiency was made in the conclusion.

The arguments presented were located principally in the discourse of the radical feminists (Spender 1982, Mahoney 1985, Lees 1987, Jones 1985). They are critical of the patriarchal structure of the education system which, they maintain, not only gives rise to sexual harassment but also subordinates and frequently negates the experiences of girls and women and adversely affects their academic performance, achievement and self-esteem. They point out how the failure of girls has frequently been attributed to factors seen as inherent in females, for example, their inability to conceptualise higher order maths (Walkerdine 1989), and call for a shift of focus to the contexts within which girls are asked to perform and to the gender bias implicit in many such contexts. Radical and socialist/Marxist feminists have paved the way for the recognition of the lack of success of women and girls as due to those societal constructs which undermine them and devalue their contributions and experiences (namely, race, sex and class oppression).

There are three interweaving themes which underpin this present study:

a. the single-sex versus mixed school debate

b. the school effectiveness debate and its contribution to developing a whole school approach

c. factors contributing to harassment and bullying in single-sex schools.

The single-sex versus mixed school debate

Research by radical feminists has revealed, for example, that in mixed schools a very high percentage of the teacher's time is spent dealing with male pupils; that work is often planned with the interests of male pupils in mind; that the resources and materials used frequently fail to acknowledge the presence and experiences of girls and women (both black and white) and that when they do, it is often in very stereotyped ways (Spender 1982).

E813 also examined the construct of masculinity in western society which forces boys and men to use girls and women as a negative reference group in order to assert their masculinity (Stanworth 1981, Mahoney 1983). It considered the fragile nature of this masculinity, which has to be constantly proven and continually earned (Chodorow 1971). Thus for radical feminists the single-sex versus co-education debate is an important one and Spender (1982) maintains that any serious commitment to alienating sexism must involve a study of single sex education as a viable alternative to the present co-educational system. Mixed schools, in the light of the experiences of girls and women in them, are viewed by many radical feminists as boys' schools with girls and women in them (Wood 1973) hence as potentially damaging for girls and women.

Arnot (1985) took the view, however, that challenging masculinity in our society does not lie simply in the single-sex versus co-education debate but in producing programmes for reducing sexism in both types of school in the short term and for removing gender as an organising variable, in the long term.

In this study I examine more closely the constructs of masculinity and femininity in our society, and how they contribute to bullying behaviour. I also challenge the argument that single-sex schooling is necessarily a safer environment for girls.

A serious omission from the discourse of the radical feminist researcher is the recognition of race and class as other organising variables which have considerable impact on the learning, performance and achievement of girls, in both mixed and single-sex schools. It may well be that girls are inhibited in the presence of boys (Sharpe 1976), which seriously affects their performance, and that they see their only options as being 'silly or silent' in this presence (Howe 1974). However, my work with schools on harassment and bullying has shown that single-sex girls' schools are also inhibiting for certain girls. It shows that these schools, in fact, do not constitute a safe, confidence-boosting learning environment for *all* girls (Burgess 1990). It shows that even in these schools some girls are forced into 'silence'.

If some feminists continue to ignore the class and race dimensions in their research and practice then not only are they presenting a distorted picture but they will continue to do untold damage to certain groups of female students

8

whose particular experiences and needs are not those of the majority and, therefore, go unrecognised and unmet. Rehana Minhas powerfully argued (1986) for the need to make very explicit the links between race, sex and class in any equal opportunities work. Hazel Taylor (1984) acknowledges the difficulties that can be experienced when trying to deal with differing forms of oppression simultaneously but concludes that it is the only way forward if we are not, in our endeavours to alleviate oppression in one area, to continue to oppress in others.

The omission of a black feminist perspective in much of the feminist debate on women's oppression has long been acknowledged (Bourne 1983) and has been addressed by both black feminists and white (Hooks 1982, Phoenix 1987, Wright 1987, Pence 1982). We cannot claim to be speaking for *all* women if issues of race, sexuality and class are not also taken on board. Therefore, when one reads such powerful statements as:

> There is convincing evidence that girls acquire in girls' schools higher self-esteem, greater self-confidence, better examination passes, especially in vital subjects, more genuine subject choice, more opportunity for leadership (Burgess 1990).

One can accept that this is perhaps the case for a greater percentage of girls than in a mixed school but it is debatable whether the above statement accurately describes the experience of all the girls in a school.

The school effectiveness debate

The acknowledgement of the importance of recognising and valuing pupil difference is also made from another theoretical perspective — that of the school effectiveness debate. Research carried out in the last twenty years into the effect that schools as institutions have on students' behaviour and scholastic achievements categorically concludes that schools do make a difference:

> In other words, to an appreciable extent children's behaviour and attitudes are shaped and influenced by their experiences at school and, in particular, by the qualities of the school as a social institution (E814 *Organisation and Professionals: Study Guide,* p. 73, Open University MA in Education Course).

Obviously this is of great importance when considering bullying behaviour in schools. Could it be that the school itself is contributing to and possibly causing bullying?

The following conclusion from the study of Rutter et al (1979) carried out in twelve inner London secondary schools, is worth quoting:

'Secondary schools in inner London differed markedly in the behaviour and attainments shown by their pupils. This was evident in the children's behaviour whilst at school, the regularity of their attendance, the proportions staying on at school beyond the legally enforced period, their success in public examinations, and their delinquency rates' (quoted in E814 *Study Guide* p.72).

Reynolds and Reid (1988) acknowledge the contributions made by studies such as Rutter et al (1979) and Reynolds (1976) to the school effectiveness debate but they also recognise that such studies belong to the 'first stage' of the research and that there is a pressing need to move to the 'second stage' so that: 'gaps in our knowledge, inadequacies in our theoretical conceptualisations and deficiencies in our methodologies will be explored in some detail' (p.169).

As stated, the 'first stage' highlighted that the informal, unstructured 'ethos' of the school was far more important in determining effectiveness, than for example, the more organisational structures. Also significant are firm leadership combined with a system of reinforcement by rewards for good behaviour rather than punishment for bad. Equally important was the highlighting of the fact that schools do make a difference; that such factors as home background, catchment area etc, whilst important, are less relevant to a child's overall achievement than what actually happens within the school (this was also acknowledged in the Report of the Commission of Enquiry chaired· by Lord Elton, *Discipline in Schools,* 1989).

So what are these 'gaps in our knowledge' that need to be addressed if we are to have a more complete picture of a school's effectiveness? I wish, at this stage, to focus on just one of the ten key areas that Reynolds and Reid (1988) have identified as requiring a more in-depth study; the need to desegregate pupils and schools. They argue that one of the major handicaps of the work to date is the practice of continuing to treat pupils as a unitary group when, in fact, American research has revealed that schools are differentially important for different groups of pupils (Coleman 1966).

We therefore need to:

analyse separately for boys and girls, older and younger pupils, higher and lower social class pupils and ethnic minority and 'host culture' children.
(Reynolds and Reid, 1988, p.174.)

This process of desegregation also needs to happen in 'the single-sex school for girls debate' if we are to acquire a truer picture of which girls these schools are effective for. Spender (1980 2nd ed) has argued that whilst the experience for girls attending girls' secondary modern schools may be demonstrably different from that of girls attending girls' grammar schools:

the fact remains that it is *only* in girls' schools that we will find conditions that are not a replication of 'real life', that is patriarchy.

I would argue further: that conditions in the girls' only secondary modern schools were indeed a replication of real life and that the girls were in the main being prepared to take up their places as working class wives and mothers in this society, with all that this entails. Teachers often had, and indeed still do have low expectations of their working class and of their black students and channel them into working class jobs.

Furthermore, the hierarchy of status attributed to subjects at all-girls schools was often one which placed those subjects traditionally associated with women and working class girls at the bottom of the ladder, for example, needlework, child care and home economics. Also, these subjects were often only available to those not deemed as clever enough to study the more 'academic' subjects (in the grammar schools), thus reinforcing the sexual division of labour in our society and teaching that those skills associated with females are not valued (Payne 1980, 2nd ed).

More recent research in Britain has concluded that certain schools are more or less effective for certain groups of pupils rather than that effective schools are effective for all the students attending them (Smith and Tomlinson 1989).

Reynolds and Reid (1988) recognise the difficulties inherent in breaking down areas of study into the kind of fine categories mentioned above but they are convinced that it must be done for a variety of reasons including: 'the need to have more sensitive descriptions of within school processes than those available at present' (p.175).

Such fine-tuning would have obvious implications for policy development. They also argue in favour of using 'teacher- researchers' as an enabling strategy.

A study of the factors contributing to harassment and bullying in single sex schools

It has already been stated that it is the radical feminist research tradition that has been primarily responsible for identifying sexual harassment within schools as one of the most oppressive forms of control in a male-structured educational system. Hence freedom from endemic sexual harassment is one of the most powerful arguments in favour of single sex schools for girls — if nothing else girls' schools are safe havens away from the prying eyes and hands of young and older males and from the vicious attacks unleashed on girls and women in the form of verbal abuse (Mahoney, 1983, Kelly and Cohn, 1988). Mahoney identified some two hundred forms of verbal abuse in her study specifically aimed at girls and women.

My study for E813 did not allow a fuller investigation into the experience of harassment of black girls, nor did it sufficiently incorporate a class analysis. Although the group of girls that I interviewed was mixed in terms of race and class, the structure of the interviews held did not allow me to pursue the sensitive issues of race and class in any great depth. For example, I was not able to have a frank discussion with the black girls involved in the interview on how race and racism as well as sexism had featured in their experiences.

Although harassment was the issue that took me into the schools for this present study, it was bullying that both schools (following an initial period of evidence gathering) decided to focus on. It would be useful here to examine the theoretical context within which bullying is located.

Bullying, although an age-old problem, is very new as an area of research:

> Bullying is the most malicious and malevolent form of deviant behaviour widely practised in our schools and yet it has received only scant attention from national and local authorities. It has failed to claim the attention of teachers' unions; our schools have given it low priority compared with disruptive behaviour and truancy; and finally it has been ignored by the educational research community (Tattum 1989).

However, the last few years have seen an increase in interest from the media, researchers, the public at large and some local education authorities (see Keise 1989 for an early account of work with the ILEA). This has been mainly due to the horrific and publicised attacks on certain individuals, which have prompted relatives to speak out and LEAs to act. The two most publicised accounts are probably those of Mark Perry, whose death as a result of bullying led his mother to establish the Anti-Bullying Campaign in conjunction with Kidscape in 1988, and the death of Ahmed Ullah at Burnage High School in 1986 (see Macdonald et. al. 1989 for a full account of the Burnage tragedy). Ahmed's death led to the extensive Macdonald Inquiry, a flurry of media attention, the anti-antiracist backlash from the Right and some action from LEAs to prevent the same thing happening in their schools. But even now action has not been extensive and the government has only very recently decided to allocate funding to Sheffield University to carry out research into bullying.

Both Mark's and Ahmed's deaths had a racist or racialist dimension and although this is not always a variable in bullying, it is a significant one. This is true, too, for this present study. We need, in fact, to be aware of the differing experiences of harassment and bullying undergone by black students and white, of working class and middle class students, for example, in order to arrive at a clearer understanding of the dynamics at play and if we are to find effective strategies for bringing about change.

There are several schools of thought and hence several definitions regarding what constitutes bullying (for example, Olweus, 1978, Lane, 1989) and part of my work with schools has been to develop with them their own working definition for their own institution. However, most definitions acknowledge an imbalance of power and hence an abuse of power (Stephenson and Smith 1989), with the powerless dominated by the powerful. It is viewed as an act which is repeated over a period of time (though Stephenson and Smith 1989 do not always consider this to be necessary), that can be physical, psychological or verbal in nature and, essentially, that causes damage and distress to the victim. Besag's definition (1989) also recognises, importantly, that bullying can also occur in the form of socially acceptable behaviour, for instance, 'in a highly competitive approach to academic, sporting or social success, which by intent, makes others feel inferior or causes distress' (p.4).

This study is particularly interested in considering the gender relations at work in bullying. I wish to consider how and why girls and boys bully — the similarities and the differences. This will have obvious implications for how this negative, destructive form of behaviour is dealt with in institutions. I shall also be considering the construct of race from both the bully and the victim's perspective and shall look at whether bullying is the same as or different from harassment. Stephenson and Smith (1989) consider their definition of bullying as: 'somewhat similar to the notion of harassment as described by Manning, Heron and Marshall (1978)' (p. 45).

The latter view harassment as a form of aggression which 'appears unprovoked, at least in the immediate situation and is directed at a person, often the same person repeatedly'.

Finally, the implications for parents, teachers, governors, institutions and LEAs are considered.

A commonly accepted distinction between harassment (either racial or sexual) and bullying is that harassment carries with it overtones of being an attack on not just an individual (as is generally the case in bullying) but on the individual's race or sex as a whole. In the words of the Swann Committee:

We believe the essential difference between racist name-calling and other forms of name-calling is that whereas the latter may be related only to the individual characteristics of a child (and would hence constitute bullying? — my question) the former is a reference not only to the child but also by extension to the family and indeed more broadly their ethnic community as a whole (Swann Report, 1985, p.35) and hence can lead to an internalisation of the accepted value judgement of the majority community by the individual which only serves 'to strengthen and perpetuate the overall climate of racism in which they find themselves' (Swann, p. 35).

In Appendix 3 of the CRE's report, *Learning in Terror* (1987) a similar distinction is made:

Insulting behaviour on the part of a pupil towards a member of a group on grounds of colour or ethnicity (or sex — my inclusion) is indefensible. It differs from other forms of adolescent verbal abuse or bullying in that it is not merely a personal attack but is aimed indiscriminately at a whole ethnic group. It is not intolerance of another's action but of another's background and culture (and/or sex — my inclusion).

The Home Office's report of the Inter-departmental Racial Attacks Group 1989) — *The Response to Racial Attacks and Harassment,* Section 2, offers a similar definition.

Chapter 3 of the *Swann Report* entitled 'Racism; Theory and Practice', paints a graphic picture of what it is like to be on the receiving end of racial harassment in Britain. Particular attention was drawn to the type of harassment experienced by the Asian community:

It was clear to us that the Asian community widely believes that it is the object of a campaign of unremitting racial harassment which it fears will grow worse in the future (p.31).

In fact, the report argues that in any school with 1% — 5% black students the situation for the black students could be intolerable and it is often so even with a higher percentage of black students.

The differing types of harassment experienced by different ethnic minority groups is obviously directly related to the perceptions that the 'host majority' have of a particular group. So that Asian students are often told that they smell, that they can't speak English or that it is alright to be called a 'Paki' because they come from Pakistan. Whereas African-Caribbean students experience racist name-calling with terms of abuse which were endemic in the 'host country's colonial and imperialist past (see Kelly, 1988 for a detailed list of the type of words used in some Manchester schools).

To suggest that racism is on the increase in the 1990s (*The Observer,* June 1990) is to imply that we have experienced a period in the past in which it had abated. This claim is, however, disputed by Swann (1985) and by the experiences of black and other ethnic minority groups in Britain during the last fifty years. However, we are experiencing a climate in the 1990s, which prevails generally in Europe, which seems to allow racism and racists to be far more visible (for example, the Secretary of State for Education, John McGregor's decision over the recent Cleveland case (1990) — to allow parents to move their child from a particular school on racist grounds).

We also need to be aware of what Swann (1985) defines as: 'feelings of negative prejudice against ethnic groups other than one's own' which 'can be found both within and between minority communities as well as between minority and majority groups' (p.27).

This type of prejudice, evidenced in certain Asian groups fighting each other, for example, Bangladeshi versus Pakistani etc. and African-Caribbeans against Asians (see *Burnage Report*, 1989) must certainly be challenged but also understood in the context of 'white racism' as the powerless seeking to gain power by either aligning with the powerful (as African-Caribbean girls in this study do with white girls against Asian girls) or by adopting an attitude of cultural superiority towards other ethnic groups (for example, the attitudes of some Chinese and Vietnamese pupils towards 'black' pupils and the animosity of certain Asian groups towards other ethnic minority communities (Swann, 1985).

The distinction made between racial and sexual harassment and bullying is important. Schools have felt it easier, in many instances, to work with the bullying label, as it is seen as one with which all students can identify, either as victim or bully (or as a bystander), at some point in their school life. Bullying in schools is seen as embracing harassment and abuse, not only on account of race, sex or class but on account of any other category of prejudice or hate as perceived by the bully at the time. It is important, however, that if we do use the bullying label we recognise its limitations in defining certain experiences (namely racial and sexual harassment) as well as its advantages. Some researchers have, in fact, used the term racial bullying to explain what is in fact harassment in schools (see Besag, 1989, p. 17). This is fine only if we are aware of the distinctions as drawn above.

A very important aspect of my work has been in revealing the number of children involved in bullying. In Lamont Girls' School some two thirds of those surveyed admitted to having been involved either as victims or as bullies. Other researchers in the field have identified figures ranging from 10% of school children to 20%-25% (Stephenson and Smith, 1989, Besag, 1989 etc) with Elliott's survey (1986) identifying as many as 38% of a sample of four thousand children.

If most children have experienced bullying, of what types are the bullying incidents and are they the same for boys and girls? Existing research suggests that boys tend to bully more than girls (Stephenson and Smith, 1989, Besag, 1989 etc.) and that when boys bully, it is often physical and results in violent, aggressive behaviour. This behaviour is often interpreted as 'boys will be boys',

15

treated as part of growing up as a male in this society and virtually accepted. There is frequently a failure to deal with bullying appropriately: as an abusive form of behaviour which can have far-reaching, long-term damaging effects. Much has been written on aggression and violence in schools (Lowenstein, 1975, Olweus, 1978, Goldstein, Apter and Harootunian, 1984) and on the issue of bullying in all-boys public schools (Walford, 1989). Evidently it is seen as an accepted and indeed integral part of the male, public school system. Interestingly, girls have been allowed to attend certain institutions in order to have a civilising effect on the boys (Swann, 1985). Bullying has also been an accepted norm in the British army.

The particular authoritarian structure of some boys' schools is seen as helping to create an aggressive, tough, macho environment which in turn condones aggression between students (Askew, 1989).

What is now becoming apparent is that bullying is also very much a feature of all-girls schools, though it often manifests itself in different ways (Tattum, 1989) and often goes unrecognised as bullying because it apparently lacks the obvious physical and aggressive element associated with male bullying behaviour.

Chapter 2
Research method

The aims of my research changed considerably during the project. When I began, as advisory teacher for gender, my intention was to assist schools to bring about institutional change in dealing with harassment and bullying. On becoming Inspector for Sex Equality in the LEA of the schools where I carried out the research, I was able to extend my aims to include developing a borough-wide focus on these issues and to assist schools even further by offering borough-wide inservice training as well as working with other officer colleagues (in consultation with institutions) on the development of policy and guidelines for dealing with harassment and bullying. It has also been possible to explore a wide range of strategies to assist institutions to deal with harassment and bullying and the management of pupil behaviour (discipline) within which these issues can be located.

My research is very much within the liberating tradition of action research, with the teacher (myself) as researcher. It is a tradition which, in terms of school-based research, has several distinct advantages. Although there are criticisms regarding the validity of such non-statistical, qualitative research, my position accords with Taylor (1984) in that:

> The great value of teacher-conducted school-focused enquiry is that it *illuminates the particular and leads to consideration of how that particular may be improved* (Millman 1987, p. 259 — my emphasis).

Action research is well suited to this investigation, particularly with its emphasis on the validity of the practitioner in the classroom observing, recording, evaluating and acting on an area identified for study; in this case harassment and bullying. Millman (1987) acknowledges a trend in LEAs of inspectors and advisers with responsibility for gender adopting the teacher-researcher model 'as a means of identifying and disseminating 'good' practice within their own authorities' (p.258). She also points out the importance of the status of the teacher-researcher as perceived by other colleagues. More seniority would indicate more influence on school policy and help to ensure that initiatives developed would be seen through. The members of staff who chaired the equal opportunities working parties at both Bankside and Lamont were members of the senior management team. And my present post certainly allows me to ensure that action around these issues takes place at a senior level in the education department.

Furthermore my work is located within that area of research aiming to examine gender as a variable in pupil behaviour and postulates that a greater understanding of this variable can influence guidelines and policy. This research focused specifically on the areas of pupil relationships (boys to boys and girls to girls) and, to a lesser extent, on that of pupils and staff, and it has implications for the development of school discipline policies within which dealing with harassment and bullying would be located. Equally important in attempting to reach a clearer understanding of such behaviour was the need to address sexism and racism as societal constructs which have a major impact on how bullying behaviour is carried out.

Thus to address the questions of what bullying is, how boys and girls bully and what the issues are for single sex schools arising out of this behaviour, required research methods that were both 'manageable and productive' (Millman 1987). I set out to be a catalyst to the schools in their work on harassment and bullying; to empower them to address the issues and to provide the theoretical underpinnings to their work. The data collection exercise involving the staff was an important part of the research because it allowed staff to look objectively at what was happening around them. The evidence collected spoke for itself and was separate from the researcher. The schools had to act not because of what the researcher said but because of what the data gathered revealed to them.

> The insights thus gained would lead to action to change where change was needed. Data was collected... examined, shared with colleagues and reflected upon. It generated discussion, recognition, amazement — and action (Millman 1987, p.259).

Action research methods are often criticised on grounds that they are not sufficiently rooted in statistical data so that their findings lack objectivity and cannot be considered valid. However, in reality action research 'draws on the widest possible range of methods, since it encompasses techniques from all the traditional methodological paradigms' (Forward 1989, p.29). It can be a skilful blend of both quantitative and qualitative research methods, so is a more interactive approach to the improvement of educational practice. Validation, in this instance, arises out of:

> the use of a range of techniques such as detailed descriptions of situations, events, people and interactions, together with the use of direct quotations, interviews and questionnaires (which are convincing) particularly when quantitative and qualitative data are juxtaposed (Forward 1989, p.34).

The qualitative aspect of the research, the interviewing of staff and students, was an essential aspect of my research. It was in this setting that I began to acquire a clearer understanding of the reality of each individual school.

Questionnaires alone would not have created this reality. Furthermore, there are inherent problems in the use of questionnaires:

> Not only did the usefulness of the findings depend on the skill with which the questionnaire had been constructed but the accuracy of the results also depended on the willingness of the respondents to complete and return the questionnaire (Millman 1987, p.262).

The schools also experienced problems in terms of the time required for collation and analysis of the responses and in the response rate (some classes at Bankside had a high degree of absenteeism on the day that the questionnaire was administered).

Like Millman, I found that:

> In contrast, 'carefully structured interviews, systematically carried out' provided more detailed information than was obtained in the written responses to questionnaires, and less structured more open-ended interviews provided room for both interviewer and interviewee to pursue new lines of inquiry and response (Millman 1987, page 262).

While it is more difficult to generalise and to quantify responses from such interviews, they serve to provide 'illuminating insights' specific to individual schools and which are so important in school-focused action research, since they determine the course of action. For example, the response of students to whether they perceived there to be a great deal of bullying in the school or not varied from 'not very much' to 'it happens all the time', depending on factors such as which class they happened to be in and whether or not they were being bullied. What the responses indicate to staff, however, is that bullying is occurring, and I would argue that no incident, once identified, should go unchallenged.

19

Chapter 3
Working with two single-sex schools

A number of schools had invited me to work with them as gender advisory teacher (with a specific brief to address racial and sexual harassment in schools). In consultation with the Inspector for Equal Opportunities (Gender), it was decided to invite selected schools to participate in what became known as 'the harassment project'.

A letter was sent to the headteachers of a number of schools in June 1989, outlining the aims of the project and detailing the specific commitment required from the participating schools. I decided that the target group with which I would work would be the schools' equal opportunities working parties, since these generally represent both 'academic' and 'pastoral' staff, and at varying levels of seniority. Also, such groups have a commitment and a brief to address equality issues within the school and, as officially recognised bodies in the school, have access to directed time for meetings. This in turn means that the working party is required to report to the headteacher and senior management on the outcomes of its work (Millman 1987). The work was thus unlikely to be marginalised and the context would be set for developing 'a whole school approach' for dealing with harassment — which I considered to be the project's main aim.

The present study details work in two single-sex secondary schools, here called Lamont Girls' School and Bankside Boys' School. The two schools are located within the local education authority for which I have subsequently (since January 1990) become the Inspector for Sex Equality — an appointment which was to have major implications for taking the work forward. However, when the project was first conceived in June 1989, a principal aim (given the very short period of two terms available to me for working with the schools) was to develop a process of working with the staff that could be continued once external support was withdrawn. My role was to be that of catalyst, to set things in motion and then withdraw. In the event the time was reduced to one term owing to my appointment as Inspector, but as Inspector I was able to maintain contact with the schools and offer advice and support, as well as monitoring and evaluating the progress of the project in the two schools.

Harassment (both racial and sexual) was viewed in both schools as a very sensitive issue. Not all staff were convinced of the need to address it and the working parties knew this. My approach was, therefore, very much within the feminist collaborative research tradition in that I tried at all times to work *with* staff. I was an outsider but an aware and empathetic outsider who could share and understand staff concerns (Griffin 1987).

Although clear about my aims, I realised that there was no one 'correct' way of achieving them. The way forward would be largely determined by the individual schools and the particular groups of teachers with whom I should be working. I did know that a heavy-handed, sledge-hammer approach could do more harm than good. I also knew that as an advisory teacher I did not have the power or status to demand a particular course of action. The two schools knew that they had problems over harassment. They wanted to focus on the causes and then identify ways to deal with them. 'The harassment project' enabled them to do just this and provided a model of working that could be used to address other issues that needed attention.

School A — Lamont Girls' School

This is an all-girls 11-16 school serving a predominantly white, English, working class catchment area. Some 25 percent of the school's intake comes from a variety of ethnic minority groups including Asian, African-Caribbean, Chinese, Turkish and Greek. A small percentage of the staff is of African-Caribbean or Asian descent.

The school welcomed my invitation to participate in the harassment project and I began working with the equal opportunities working party in September 1989. The working party was already well aware of the level of racial harassment within the school and felt that the project would offer the school a clear structure for addressing it. All members of the group were female and white and ranged in experience from probationary to senior teachers.

I envisaged three or four sessions at most with the group during the autumn term. This would allow us to explore and identify the main issues of concern and set the agenda for a whole-school focus for the spring term (when I knew that my support would be withdrawn). In the event, there were four sessions: three twilight sessions from 4-6pm, and the fourth a half day from 2-5pm.

The first session outlined the aims of the project and set the focus on harassment in a much wider national context. The Elton report on *Discipline in Schools* (1989) and *The Burnage Report* (1989) documenting the inquiry into the racist murder in 1986 of Ahmed Ullah, a pupil at Burnage High School, meant that harassment and particularly, racial harassment was receiving a great deal of attention in the media. LEAs were beginning to respond. The ILEA had swiftly identified harassment as an issue of great concern, aware that a Burnage-like situation could all too easily arise in any one of its schools. The ILEA's response echoed a paragraph in *The Burnage Report:*

Could it happen again? Could it have happened before? How many head teachers in Manchester and other parts of the United Kingdom on hearing about the tragedy did not have cause to look about them and say 'There, but for fortune, go I' (p. 245).

Staff at Lamont School had long recognised that harassment was a problem — it was about how to deal with it that the school felt unsure. They feared that any direct action might make a bad situation worse but did not realise that what made things worse was doing nothing. (This reaction was common in many of the schools with which I had contact. It was often mistakenly assumed that naming the problem explicitly would only exacerbate matters, and some staff were eager to point out that they had had no problem until the school chose to raise the issue. When, in fact, raising the issue had probably given confidence to those being harassed to speak out for the first time.)

It was important, in the introductory session, to make clear that addressing harassment was not merely a marginal issue, which would divert much needed attention and time from the real job in hand, that is, delivering the National Curriculum. The two are inextricibly linked. The government is emphatic that the National Curriculum is an entitlement curriculum. Yet how are students to acquire full access to this curriculum if they are suffering harassment, harassment which is ignored by those in authority?

In its *Implementing the National Curriculum — an Inset Pack*, the ILEA stated clearly that:

> Confident participation is a pre-requisite for achievement. Confident participation relates to self-image, teacher attitude and expectation, student aspiration, the content, image and language in learning materials, classroom organisation and teaching methods *together with an environment free from harassment. Factors which cause differentiation in pupil performance in terms of gender and race have to be identified and addressed if the national curriculum objectives are to be attained* (my emphasis).

These objectives include promoting 'the spiritual, moral, cultural, mental and physical development of pupils at the school and of society' and the preparation of 'pupils for the opportunities, responsibilities and experiences of adult life' (NCC — *A Curriculum For All*).

If these objectives are to be realised, harassment and bullying must be strenuously combated by schools and society. We know that the lives of many people in this society are plagued by incidents of racial and sexual harassment (see *Living in Terror,* (CRE, 1987) and *The Response to Racial Attacks and Harassment* (Home Office, 1989). We also know that more needs to be done to address these problems and that this will necessitate a much closer liaison between education and other agencies such as housing and social services. Harassment and bullying are not confined within the school gates.

At the end of the first session the members of the working party were asked to carry out an evidence-gathering exercise around the school and to report their findings to the next session. Guidance sheets from the *Gender Equality: From Analysis to Action* pack (1989) helped them to decide which areas of the school to focus on. Staff decided to focus primarily on groupings of pupils in classrooms and assemblies, language, participation of students in lessons and seating arrangements. The chair of the working party also agreed to carry out a review of racist incidents reported in the school.

Their findings are described in chapter 4. These findings identified racial bullying as a clear expression of the degree and extent of racism within the school. Many Asian girls were teased, ostracised and verbally and physically abused and responded by trying to be as invisible as possible in the classroom — with serious consequences for their learning. An extreme example (Case Study D) concerned one Asian girl who, after repeated bullying by some of her white classmates, had become ill and a poor attender and was no longer attending the school.

The cycle of underachievement caused by fear, lack of confidence, absenteeism, low self-esteem (as depicted in Lamont's analysis of bullying sheet, in Chapter 4) was now becoming very clear. At the third meeting in October 1989, when the findings were analysed, a half-day session was arranged for the working party to explore bullying as a concept more thoroughly and to begin to look at how the issue could be raised with other staff and students.

During that final half-day session for the term, held in November, the members of the working party achieved a shared common understanding of bullying and were able to develop their own definition of bullying at Lamont School which they would subsequently take to the rest of the staff:

> Bullying at Lamont School is the use of physical or verbal aggression to establish power and/or instil fear and to divert attention from something the bully is possibly unhappy about in themselves. It is often racist/classist in origin and can involve the following:
>
> pushing/shoving/hitting
> isolating another person
> ridicule
> 'it's only a joke'
> making personal comments about someone's looks, size, gender, colour, race, background.

An incident is identified as bullying if the victim perceives it as bullying. By exploring case studies of bullying through role-play and discussion, the group identified possible strategies for dealing with incidents of bullying. The session worked well. What was clear from the participants' comments was 'the need to 'recognise' and 'own' that bullying happens' and 'the need to set up the mechanism for facing and dealing with it'. The members of the working party were now aware that their own inability to acknowledge bullying when it happened meant that they were in effect colluding with the bullies and that even when action had been taken it often made the situation worse for the victim. (For example, suspending the bullies gained them more support from their class-mates, who also frequently rounded on the victim. Or moving the victim to another group — which the bully regarded as a sign of success on her part.)

After this session, the working party felt empowered to take their under-standing to the rest of the staff and into their classrooms, where they could work on it with students. A 90-minute INSET session for the whole staff was planned for the start of the spring term (January 1990). Led by the members of the working party, it allowed staff to explore and define bullying, to look at case studies, devise a questionnaire for students to complete and to plan an introduc-tory lesson on bullying for use in class. Subsequently all students in years seven to ten completed the questionnaire. The chair of the working party (the main link between the school and myself) collated the responses and summarised the findings in the form of a spidergram (see Chapter 4). Significantly, two thirds of the students who had completed the questionnaire said that they had been involved in bullying either as victim or bully. The findings were then discussed in tutor groups.

Since this initial focusing on bullying, the chair of the working party continues to monitor incidents of bullying within the school. Teachers bring in bullying as a theme in their work (notably English and PSE) and it is reported that there is now a far more 'open climate' in the school, that is, one in which bullying can be discussed.

The chair has worked with members of the school's year council in the summer term to draft a school anti-harassment charter, to be taken to the rest of the school in the new term. The working group believes that ways still need to be found to involve parents and support staff. I continue to support and advise the school in my new role as Inspector for Sex Equality, and I consider that the school has, in this year, shifted considerably in its thinking and practice but that much still needs to be done. In July 1990, ten months after the project began, the chair of the working party completed a questionnaire to assist me in evaluating the project (Chapter 4) and I interviewed three students from years nine and ten.

The school is committed to continuing to tackle bullying, working mostly through the curriculum and continuing to develop awareness. I arranged for all secondary schools in the borough to have access to the Neti Neti theatre company's production *Only Playing Miss* (Casdagli, 1990) and to two workshops with the company. The play, which deals with the theme of bullying, is an impressive production in three languages (English, Bengali and sign language) and has been widely acclaimed. I still liaise with the schools to ensure that follow-up work takes place. Ideally I would like to see work on harassment and bullying clearly identified as a target within each school's Institutional Development Plan, accompanied by a detailed plan of action specifying how the school will develop a whole-school approach for dealing with it.

School B — Bankside Boys' School

Bankside in an all-boys, 11-18 school with approximately 1,200 on roll. The school serves a racially mixed catchment area, although the predominant ethnic group is white English. A recently appointed male headteacher and a newly appointed senior management team (in 1988) are committed to challenging and changing the rather intimidating, aggressive and competitive ethos for which the school is known. They aim to create an ethos where the emphasis is directed towards addressing the needs of the individual within the context of a management style which is less authoritarian and more open, democratic and consultative.

This has not always been easy, particularly as some of the 'old guard' are keen to maintain and preserve the old traditions. As advisory teacher for equal opportunities (gender) I had already, early in the spring term of 1989, made contact with the chair of the equal opportunities working party, and knew that many female members of staff were extremely concerned about the level of sexual harassment of women staff in the school and what seemed like the school's inability to address this issue satisfactorily. They also complained bitterly of the generally sexist behaviour and attitudes of some male students and colleagues and felt that the present coping strategies only served to undermine what they perceived as their limited authority.

Bankside was invited to take part in the harassment project in the summer term of 1989. The head teacher was keen for the school to become involved and agreed that the equal opportunities working party should commit its scheduled meetings for the year to addressing a whole-school approach for dealing with harassment.

I began working with the school in the autumn term of 1989. As with Lamont School, the time schedule was extremely tight. I offered to work with the group on identifying the issues, developing strategies and more importantly on empowering the group to take the work forward. Each of the two sessions ran for approximately two hours, after school. We drew up a similar programme to that offered to Lamont School.

The first meeting in September 1989 looked at the expectations of the group and began to identify forms of harassment within the school. The working party highlighted the sexual harassment of female staff as an ongoing cause for concern and acknowledged other forms of unacceptable pupil behaviour (including name-calling, graffiti, racial harassment, bullying and physical violence). At the end of the first session, members of the working party were asked to collect examples of harassment, using as a guide sheets from the Coventry document, *Gender Equality: From Analysis to Action* 1989.

At the second meeting a month later, the group reported their findings verbally, confirming the forms of harassment previously identified but also clearly specifying the level and nature of bullying in the school. It was decided at this meeting that the initial focus of attention would be on bullying. What had become swiftly apparent was the all-pervasive and damaging nature of this form of behaviour and it seemed strategically sensible to begin to address a form of harassment with which all students could readily identify. A process for dealing more effectively with sexual harassment would follow.

My subsequent contact with Bankside was through the deputy head teacher with responsibility for year seven and year eight students, since the school had decided to focus initially on the lower school. However, I also maintained contact with the deputy head teacher who is a member of the equal opportunities working party and who has oversight of the development of the school's sexual harassment policy and guidelines, to which a group of female members of staff were committed.

With the lower school deputy head, a programme was devised for the remainder of the autumn term involving my working with the tutors of years seven and eight for part of a staff training day. The aim was to develop awareness of the issues and to produce a questionnaire on bullying to be completed by all the students in years seven and eight. It was also agreed that I would take an assembly for the lower school, in which I would launch the anti-bullying project.

At the start of the training day I met with some reluctance and scepticism from some tutors, who felt that they were inadequately trained to deal with the issue. Others wanted clear guidelines thrashed out for dealing with bullying incidents before they could proceed. Still others felt that handling the issue wrongly would only make things worse, so wanted to leave things as they were for the time being. It was necessary to point out that generally it was precisely 'doing nothing' that made a bad situation worse, that we were merely making a start and that whatever was planned would be tried out and revised until satisfactory procedures were established.

By the end of the training day, tutors had prepared a draft questionnaire and outlined a brief programme to cover three tutorial periods. By the end of the third, the results of the questionnaire would be collated and students would begin suggesting strategies for addressing bullying. The school council would use these suggestions when drafting a school policy.

The students listened attentively to what I had to say at the assembly, and the first two tutorial periods went well. However, not all tutors collated their questionnaires, so were not equipped for the third tutorial lesson, when students were to start discussing how to deal with incidents.

Six months after the project began and three months after students had completed their questionnaires, the deputy head teacher reported sadly to me that cohesion had been lost because certain tutors had not co-operated fully with the project. And when he realised how much work was still needed with the school council regarding its role, he had to abandon the original plan to begin to develop strategies with the council.

On the positive side, however, the lower school students were much more aware and much quicker to report incidents of bullying and seek help. In fact, when the deputy head was reporting to me his evaluation of the project to date later in that term, we were twice interrupted in the space of an hour by students wanting his help because they were being bullied! It might have been extremely useful to interview the year tutors to find out why some of them had been unable or unwilling to follow the work through with the students, but I did not have time.

Ten months after the start of the project, the deputy head organised a follow-up questionnaire for the students in years seven and eight, using a slightly different format that allowed for easier collation. The aim was to ascertain how students felt about bullying in the school following the fairly high profile it had received during the year.

Nearly half the respondents reported that bullying had become less frequent; others said it had remained the same. A significant minority reported that there had been an increase. By far the most frequent types of bullying identified by the students were cussing (verbal abuse), hitting and taking money (in that order). Being 'sent to Coventry' was not signalled, because this had not been included as a category on the questionnaire, yet staff knew that this happened to a significant number of students. An alarming two thirds of the respondents to the questionnaire stated that they had been bullied at one time or another, while a significant number stated that they themselves had at some time bullied others.

Most bullying took place at school, although the toilets, a site of bullying in much of the literature, were not a key area. Where the bullying is actually happening in school is still unclear. Most of the bullying was reported as coming from older boys from other years and other houses — which has obvious implications for supervision. Students reported bullying to friends and parents first of all, followed by their head of house, another teacher or the head or a deputy head teacher and, last of all, the form tutor. Just over a third said there was some bullying in the school whilst another third reported that there was a lot of bullying.

Towards the end of the summer term (1990), I interviewed three students from year eight to obtain student perceptions of bullying and these are discussed in Chapter 5. To give a directed focus to the interviews, I used a set of questions but also asked others when appropriate. Some of the boys questioned understood the issues better than others and were more articulate and forthcoming, but all were valuable as the perceptions of an individual. All three had been or still were victims, and the importance for victims of being listened to and having credence given to their experiences cannot be too heavily stressed. Schools have, in my view, a commitment to the well-being of each member of the student body, and every case of bullying should be treated seriously.

Chapter 4
Lamont Girls' School:
Gathering the Evidence

Chapter 4 is a collection of data concerning Lamont Girls' School. It contains research instruments and questionnaires, and charts the pupils replies. It records the responses of one teacher to the project and ends with the case studies of three girls who were bullied and a brief account of one of the pupils' own strategies for overcoming bullying and harassment in the school.

Analysis of Bullying as it goes on in Lamont School
Issues identified:

Racial Harassment

Groups in class
(classroom organisation)

Bullying

verbal abuse — (racist comments, name-calling, comments on dress, accent etc)

Names
(misspelt/mispronounced)

Physical abuse (pushing, shoving, slapping)

Timetabling

Ostracism/isolation

Outcomes

Canteen/support staff training

Mechanisms for reporting incidents

Curriculum content (issues not being explained because of fear of student reaction)

Suspensions/exclusions
(conditions of)

mixed ability teaching and Differentiated learning

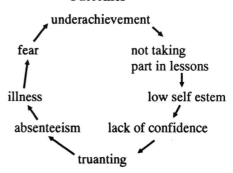

underachievement

fear

not taking part in lessons

illness

low self estem

absenteeism

lack of confidence

truanting

Evaluation by participants of school-based training day on bullying and harassment

What I found most useful today was:

Discussing the topic, airing views with other like-minded people — deciding strategies.
Having the time and space to focus my mind on one particular issue and to work through it systematically.
Discussion and sharing of opinions about situations.
Having a decent length of time to clarify and bring together what is actually happening in school — to identify issues.

What I did not find useful was:

Time limits.

The practical ideas I will use back in my classroom and around the school are:

Clarify the behaviour — distinguish between the behaviour and the person (bullying behaviour) — importance of taking action — supporting the victim — listening to both victim and bully.
Possibly looking at case studies and getting discussion around them.
Case Studies
Awareness of situations
Case Studies — Role play

The issues that have been raised for me are:

The need to 'recognise' and own that bullying happens.
The need to set up the mechanism of facing and dealing with it.
Need for monitoring incidents.
School lack of policy on bullying
School putting responsibility on parent if bullying happens outside of school.
My own inattention to some case of bullying.

Recording and monitoring of bullying
Supporting parents
The crucial importance of a whole-school policy with clear procedures re bullying.
Need for Parent Support Group.

Where does it take place?

dinner ⌐   ⌐   due to time factors
tuckshop | queues |
biscuit ⌐   ⌐   inadequate organisation
when there are fewer teachers around (a supervisory problem)
in classrooms, even when teachers are present
on the way home/around where they live
in the market
'outside the gate'

Recording and monitoring

all fights should be recorded
exclusions/suspensions should be monitored for bullying
a named individual with overall responsibility for monitoring and recording.

What I think could have been improved on is:

More time!

I would like a further session on:

How to interest other staff
Actually forming a school policy where we identify clearly what particular actions are unacceptable and how we will move towards making Lamont an open, 'telling' school.
1. How to feed back information to staff
2. How to incorporate information into PSE programme
Need to involve pupils and parents and to raise awareness

Any further comments

This term's work has been well structured and interesting and hopefully will continue
Thanks for information, providing format as a forum for us. Appreciate the *practical* things we've done
I thoroughly enjoyed the session and gained a lot from it.

The Questionnaire to Lamont Pupils

BULLYING

1) Have you ever been bullied? YES NO
   When
   What happened?
   What did you do?

2) Have you ever been a bully? YES NO
   What did you do?
   When did you do it?
   Why did you do it?

3) What do you think is the best thing school can do about bullies?

Lamont School:
Researcher's interview questions to pupils

1. Do you think there is a lot of bullying in this school? If yes, why? If no, why not?
2. Who is mainly effected? Do you think the school should try to stop it? If yes, why? If no, why not?
3. Have you ever been bullied?
4. Where? Why? How?
5. For how long?
6. What did you do about it? Tell parent/teacher/friend — if not, why not?
7. How did it make you feel?
8. What would you have liked the school to do about it?
9. What actually happened?
10. How do girls/boys generally bully?
11. Why do girls/boys bully?
12. Do you think there are differences in the way boys and girls bully?
13. Have you ever bullied?
14. If yes, Why? How? Where?
15. For how long?
16. How did it make you feel?
17. Are you still bullying now? If no, what made you stop? If yes, why?
18. What action did the school take?
19. Was it appropriate?
20. Do you think bullies should be helped? If yes, what help do you think should be given to children who bully?
21. What 3 things would help you to cope better next year (i.e. what would you like school/home to do?)
22. Has there been an improvement in bullying at the school this year? If yes, why?
23. Does much bullying take place outside of school?
24. Have you heard of Childline? Samaritans? Would you turn to them for help?
25. Is there anything else you would like to add?

BULLYING

BULLYING IS — POWER — WHEN SOMEONE IS CRUEL or HORRIBLE
— PUTTING PEOPLE DOWN — BLANKING

IS — ISOLATING — SINGLING OUT

INTOLERANCE — RACISM — SEXISM — SIZISM — DISCRIMINATION

PAINFUL, POINTLESS

TAKING MONEY

HIDING PEOPLE'S PROPERTY

FOR BEING CLEVER

BEING PICKED ON

HIT / NAME CALLING

BEATING SOMEONE UP FOR NO REASON

VIOLENCE — DANGEROUS
— PHYSICAL

INTIMIDATION

MENTAL — VERBAL

MAKING SOMEONE'S LIFE HELL — MAKING PEOPLE AFRAID

HAVE YOU EVER BEEN BULLIED?

One girl held me, the other hit me, told me to cover the face, I'd stay in, not go out.

They started saying we were poor.

Someone said something horrible about my mum.

She pulled my hair and called me name, kicked me.

I twisted my ear and punched me.

Hit my head on a table, beats me up.

My brother/sister

I was forced to give a necklace to fight,
to tell a lie to the police
to give money
to hit her or be bullied.

I couldn't speak English so people from my class bullied me.

I was constantly provoked by a small and numerous were spread which offended my self-esteem went a little.

Pulled me and caught me about my clothes.

Took my bag and threw it through the window, she used to take my bag away.

They hid my work and coat in the toilets, called me names, they called me 'fatty' and stuff like that.

They said I was ugly also my face was scarred and they hated me.

I was beaten up badly and they stole my chain.

I was called racist names and made to feel different.

He called me Paki and spat on me.

The person bullied me because I was Turkish.

I was called racist names and made to feel different.

HAVE YOU EVER BEEN A BULLY?

- I pick on people younger than me because I was picked on.
- I called her names and made her life hell, to make me look big, feel great.
- I was upset and took my spite out on her.
- I kept pushing her everywhere she said her.
- I swore at her most of the time.
- I asked them horrible questions
- I did it to make me feel better.
- I hit her because she was annoying me.
- I called her names because other people did it.
- I picked on her because of her reath.
- I chose someone as helpless as I was –
- I called her names because she smelled and I had nothing else to do.
- I called them names because they were different from us –
- I beat up people I don't like because I don't like them.
- I beat up my nephews and niece because they get on my nerves.
- I watched and helped someone get beaten up.
- I joined in with the bullies –
- She was a bit and the class was together.

Charter Against Forms of Harassment

1. *Lamont pupils and staff agree that bullying will not be tolerated*

2. *An atmosphere will be created that makes us a 'telling and listening' school*

3. *Incidents of bullying will be taken seriously and dealt with immediately*

4. *People who are bullied will be supported, each incident recorded and the action taken recorded.*

5. *Parents/guardians of the those involved will be informed*

6. *The bully will be counselled — if necessary moved to another class — not the person bullied.*

7. *The staff and School Council to review the charter each June.*

Case Studies from Lamont School

Student A — Sally — white, middle class, year nine student. Articulate and with a deep awareness of bullying and its consequences.

Sally maintained that there is a great deal of bullying in the school. She had personally experienced it in her own class, sees it happen in other year groups and witnessed a bullying incident at least once a week. In her experience girls were bullied mainly because of their race, culture, class, accent, size — and for what sometimes seemed like no reason at all. She felt that the teachers were strong on challenging racism but that they did not always see what was happening. She could not understand bullying and felt it was stupid and wrong. She herself had been bullied by four girls in her class. There had been no physical violence but a great deal of name-calling, personal comments — 'she thinks she's posh', 'she's such a bitch' — and dirty looks. On one occasion she had been followed in the streets. The bullying had been going on for most of the academic year (1989 – 1990) and blew up out of an argument she had had with a close friend. Somehow the rest of the class had then become involved.

Sally finally confided in her mother, whom she had not wanted to involve. However, when Sally started being followed in the streets, her mother came to the school to complain and the teachers dealt with the bullies. The harassment has since died down.

The experience, however, had been disempowering. Sally felt that she could not look over to the other side of the room during lessons to where the bullies sat. She could not retaliate by name-calling because it was alien to her: the names and comments hurt and depressed her. Although the school appeared to sort it out well once they knew about it, Sally felt that she should not have had to go through the experience. She felt that teachers needed to be made aware that there is a lot of bullying going on.

When asked about the ways in which girls bully, Sally replied that it tended to be through being 'bitchy', by swearing, through name-calling and by giving dirty looks. They did sometimes fight but less than boys (Kelly and Cohn's reports (1988) and the BBC2 programme *40 Minutes — 'Bullies'* draw the same conclusions). Sally would like to see the school offering sessions which would allow students to open up about bullying. She thought that the bullies did not always realise that they were bullying.

Student B — Pratibha — year ten student frequently bullied but will stand up for herself.

Pratibha was emphatic that there was a great deal of bullying in the school. She had experienced it since her first year and quite regularly saw others being bullied. She felt that it was mainly the Asian girls who were bullied, particularly those like herself, who tried to stand up for themselves. She could not recall having seen any white girls being bullied.

She felt the bullying was racist. She was often called 'Paki' as well as 'slag', 'tart', 'bitch'. Girls would push into her when walking past, so as to start an argument, and generally follow this by hitting. If she ignored the abuse, the bullies would try something else. She has found the current year to be by far the worst so far: she has been badly beaten up twice this year, and was still quite badly bruised in the face when I interviewed her. In one attack she had been punched in the nose so violently that she thought at first it was broken, and was unable to attend school for a week. However, she is perhaps less bothered by the bullying now than when she was bullied in her first year, even though she was not beaten then — offering the explanation that 'I have got used to it'.

After the first beating, two girls were suspended for three days. Pratibha felt the rest of the class turned against her because of these suspensions (she said, 'it felt like the whole school') accusing her of suspending the girl and calling her names. It was this that led to the second attack, in an empty classroom after school. As a result of this second attack Pratibha had to see her doctor yet again. The next day the main bully, an African-Caribbean girl, was suspended for three days and once again the other girls turned against her, including the bully's sister, blaming her for the bully's exclusion. It seemed to her that the whole school knew of the incident because girls from other years and classes kept coming up and asking her: 'Are you Pratibha?'

The excluded bully has since returned to school. Pratibha does not regard a temporary exclusion as a viable form of punishment or a solution to the problem of bullying, since bullies generally like being out of school. For her own part, she feels she is in a 'no win' situation. She does try to stand up for herself but this simply makes things worse. She categorically maintains that she would never bully because she knows how it feels.

When asked if she though the bullies should be helped, she said she did not know. Nor could she understand why African-Caribbean girls joined in with the white bullies. She could only conclude that maybe it was because 'they think Asian girls aren't modern that they should forget their culture'.

Pratibha reported that she felt the school often acted in a racist way over the bullying of Asian girls. When incidents are reported, for example, some staff choose not to take any action while others have made comments to her such as 'Why does it always happen to you, Pratibha?' In fact she felt that the school had only really taken decisive action in her own case after her social worker intervened. At the end of the interview, Pratibha told me she was dreading a meeting after school that day with the bully, the bully's parents and the form tutor. When I asked why, she replied 'Because Monica (the bully) is tough.' (One

41

does indeed question the wisdom of setting up an interview which puts the victim in what seems to be a very vulnerable position).

Student C — Linda — white, working-class year nine student. Linda has experienced bullying both as a victim and a bully.

Unlike Sally and Pratibha, Linda did not think there was much bullying in the school — that is, she herself had not seen much going on. She acknowledged that there was, however, a substantial amount of bullying of Asian girls — 'probably because they dress differently' and 'are too frightened to tell the teacher'. However, in her own class it was 'only comments, no really serious bullying'. She also felt that girls who came from a different country and quiet girls who did not answer back were targets for bullies.

Linda admitted to having been bullied herself for about two weeks earlier in the year. The bullying had occurred in her class and involved girl who had previously been a friend. Linda was subjected to name-calling and hurtful comments. Swift intervention by teachers who saw what was happening had prevented it from developing further and Linda's mother had helped by coming to the school. Again as with Sally and Pratibha, the incident made her feel that everyone knew about it and, in her case, made her more withdrawn. She was convinced that 'bitchiness' was the main feature in the bullying behaviour of girls, whereas boys bullied in much rougher ways.

Linda admitted to having bullied an Asian girl at her primary school. She had done so because of her different nationality, making 'bitchy' remarks about the way the girl looked and dressed. She said she would not bully anyone now, because she knew from her own recent experience how it felt to be bullied. She had not been aware of the primary school having taken any action at the time. She felt that one way to deal with bullies was to make them experience what it feels like.

The 'Bully Line'

A discussion with a group of girls from another local girls' school demonstrates clearly how bullying transcends class, race and creed. Anyone can be a target. Of the five girls I interviewed, three had been subjected to bullying. One of the girls who had been viciously bullied decided to establish a 'bully line' in the school. The line is simply a befriending mechanism but is proving to be a very effective strategy for offering support to victims. Any girl in the school who is being bullied need no longer be frightened to talk about the experience.

The members of the 'bully line' are available to be contacted and will befriend the victim (who they know from their own experiences is often isolated and friendless and hence a target for bullying) and mediate with staff.

This simple strategy had worked effectively for one of the girls in the group. She had been 'rescued' by other girls in her class, who saw what was happening and decided to do something about it. They noticed her isolation and fear and resolved not to stand by and ignore it but to befriend her.

Chapter 5
Bankside Boys' School:
questionnaires and case studies

This chapter contains similar data to the previous chapter on Lamont School, gathered during the time that the project ran at Bankside School.

The Questionnaire

Please do *not* put your name on this sheet.

Answer all questions by putting a circle round the letter. You may circle more than one letter for all the questions apart from number one, two and three.

1. Since Christmas has the amount of bullying:

    a. become less
    b. remained the same
    c. increased?

2. Have you ever been bullied?

    a. yes
    b. no
       If you answer no, go to question 9

3. If you have answered yes to question 2, have you been bullied

    a. rarely
    b. sometimes
    c. frequently?

4. How were you bullied? Was it:

    a. taking your money (stealing)
    b. taking your possessions (e.g. your pen)
    c. hitting
    d. cussing (name calling)
    e. other?

5. Where were you bullied

    a. at school
    b. in the area where you live

c. on your way to and from school
d. in the toilets?
(If you have not been bullied at school, leave this blank)

6. Who is doing the bullying? Is it someone/some people

a. in your tutor group
b. in your house
c. in your year
d. in another year (circle the year 1,2,3,4,5,6)
e. in another house (circle the house B,G,M,O,R,Y)?

7. Did you tell any of the following that you were being bullied:

a. a friend
b. your form teacher
c. another teacher
d. your Head of House
e. the Head or Deputy Head
f. your parents?

8. Have you ever bullied?

a. yes
b. no
   If your answer is no, please go to question 10

9. Where did you bully someone else? Was it:

a. at school
b. outside school
c. at a previous school?

10. Do you think there is:

a. little bullying at this school
b. some bullying here
c. a lot of bullying here?

Case Studies From Bankside School

Student A — Joseph — small, quietly spoken African boy.
Joseph felt that there was quite a lot of bullying in the school, mainly older boys beating up younger, smaller boys. He himself had been bullied quite badly on one occasion by another boy in his class (whom the deputy head teacher identified as a known National Front supporter). Joseph recalled being hit violently in the stomach by the other boy, for what seemed to him to be no apparent reason. Although it only happened once, Joseph identified the attack as a bullying attack. He reported the incident to the class teacher, who alerted one of the deputy heads. The bully was excluded for two weeks and has since left school. Asked how the attack made him feel, Joseph replied simply 'sad'. He felt that boys generally bullied in physically aggressive ways, for example, kicking, hitting and beating up. He could not explain why people bullied and did not think that bullies should necessarily be helped. But he was adamant that they should be made to stop their bullying behaviour.

Student B — Sanjay — a very small, quiet, timid-looking Asian boy.
Sanjay felt that bullying occurred frequently at the school; particularly boys extorting money from other boys. This had happened to him on a number of occasions. He recalled being bullied for money both in school and outside. Usually the bullying was in the form of a threat: 'Gimme your money or I'll beat you up' and this was no idle threat. Since the first year, he had been bullied by the same boy in his class. This year the bully had joined forces with another classmate and so Sanjay is now being threatened by two boys in his class. He has reported the bullying to his teachers and the bullies have been put on report. Sanjay felt that although his own parents knew he was being bullied, they were too busy to come to the school.

He vividly recalled how the bullying had begun in his first year. Jason, an African-Caribbean boy, accused Sanjay of taking a pen which he claimed was the one he had lost. He threatened Sanjay with an ultimatum: 'Give me the money or buy me a new pen.' Since then Jason has several times taken Sanjay's dinner money — sometimes by actually putting his hands into Sanjay's pockets. The other boys see what is happening but, Sanjay feels, are too frightened to do anything about it. The bullying made him feel both guilty and scared. He would like to see Jason removed from the class and the school should take immediate action if he still continued to bully. He did not think that there had been any improvement regarding bullying in the school this year but said that he still liked the school.

47

Student C — John — a white student of average height and build but with disabled legs which affect his balance and gait.

John was articulate and aware and showed a clarity of insight which seemed way beyond his years. John felt that he had not seen a great deal of bullying around the school, though he personally had experienced it on several occasions because of his disability. Bullies, he felt, attacked anyone they perceived as different from themselves. The boys who seemed to be mainly on the receiving end of bullying were the ones who wore glasses, boys of a different race, boys who were either too fat or too skinny and anyone with a disability. John has been bullied since the first year but feels that it happens far less frequently now. He received a great deal of verbal abuse regarding his disability — often from classmates but out of the hearing of the teacher. However, John was very adamant about not letting such remarks pass: 'I won't tolerate it' he said. He made a point early on in his first year of reporting the attacks to his head of house, who responded swiftly by coming into the tutor group and addressing the class. John recalled his words, 'If you carry on like this you will have me to deal with and I'll not be as nice as John'. John admires his head of house, whom he describes as 'a nice, listening person. That's the sort of teacher I like'.

John also recalled a more recent incident. A school keeper had said to him as he walked past: 'Go and get your legs and eyes sorted out'. This time John went straight to the head teacher, who treated the incident very seriously. 'The teachers in this school will not tolerate any messing about' John said emphatically.

John also mentioned a couple of incidents where he felt that some teachers had also bullied, pushing him intentionally, so that he lost his balance. Staff are aware that John's disability causes problems with his balance. Again, his head of house had dealt with the incident.

Asked how the bullying made him feel, John replied, 'Strange. It made me feel abnormal — something that shouldn't be here'. When I asked if there was anything else that he would like the school to do, he replied: 'The school has done enough. They've done all they could do'.

Common forms of bullying in the school identified by John were: taking money, pushing and verbal abuse — particularly concerning each other's parents. He felt that students bullied for a variety of reasons such as jealousy over something the victim owns, or because their own parents treat them badly and they take their anguish out on others, or because they do not understand that someone with a disability can fight back. They always pick on those they think are weaker than themselves. John was willing to give the bullies the benefit of the doubt but felt that if they continued after they were told to stop then they should be permanently excluded.

John wanted to see the staff at the school getting together to discuss ways to help the bullies. He was excited about a recent video his class had been involved in making with the Neti Neti Theatre Company, which had recently held two workshops in the school on bullying. John and the other boys involved had improvised a scene on racial bullying. John concluded by saying, 'I think this can be the worst kind of bullying'.

Chapter 6
The research findings and their implications

This chapter examines the outcomes and implications of my findings under the following headings:

a. Lamont Girls' School

b. Bankside Boys' School

c. The gender and race implications of bullying and harassment in single sex schools

From the analysis by staff of questionnaires submitted to students at both schools, some two thirds of all those questioned appear to have been involved in bullying at some time. This figure is commensurate with wider studies carried out in other parts of the country. In fact, Pat Lister in the BBC 2 programme, *40 Minutes — Bullies* (November 1989) maintained that Britain has possibly the highest incidence of bullying in Western Europe. Kelly's research commissioned as part of *The Burnage Report,* found that:

> One of the first things we learnt from the survey is that being teased and bullied is a common experience: at least two thirds of the students in each school, both boys and girls, stated that they had been teased or bullied at school (Kelly and Cohn, 1988, p.12).

Furthermore, name-calling in particular, and physical violence, were identified as two of the most pervasive forms of bullying and harassment in the Kelly and Cohn studies. They and other studies reveal — as does the world of literature — that the reasons for bullying are extensive and seemingly endless. Adrian Mitchell says it all in his poem 'Back in the Playground Blues' (1984):

> Well you get it for being Jewish
> And you get it for being black
> Get it for being chicken
> And you get it for fighting back
> You get it for being big and fat
> Get it for being small
> Oh those who get it get it and get it
> For any damn thing at all.

Whilst the present paper acknowledges the need to identify who the victims are and who the bullies are, it does not offer a detailed analysis of the different types of personalities that may be classified as victim or bully. Readers are referred to studies by Besag (1989), Stephenson (1967) and Smith (1989). We can, however, learn much about the main types of victim and bullying behaviour as identified from the questionnaires completed by the students at Lamont and Bankside schools. We also consider the implications of such findings for the schools, the parents, the LEA and the community at large.

Research findings and their Implications for Lamont Girls' School

From Chapter 4 we can note the different types of bullying identified by the students questioned at Lamont School. Although each form of bullying appears painful and demeaning to victims and requires swift and skilful action, it is racist bullying that the members of the school's equal opportunities working party found to be most damaging in both its extent and its nature. Racist bullying not only affects the individual but has wider and far-reaching implications for interracial community strife. Kelly (1988) compares the use of the abusive term 'specky-four-eyes' with 'Paki' or 'Nigger' and concludes that:

> It is part of the same vocabulary and less frequently used than words such as 'Paki' and 'Nigger' which are not only personally insulting, but which can also be used to excite racial tensions.

She warns that:

> Until and unless students and teachers draw some lines of demarcation between the two kinds of name-calling, the vocabulary of racial names will continue to be prominent in schools and will feed into the dynamics of relations between the racial groups (p. 283).

Staff at Lamont had already in their findings reported the extent of racist name-calling. For example, one teacher recalled that when she allowed an Asian student to leave the class first because she was one of few girls ready, several white students commented loudly 'She's let the Paki out', 'She's a Paki lover'. It is difficult even to begin to imagine what such a student must feel, having to live her life with such verbal abuse an almost daily threat. Yet this is the inescapable reality for many Asian students in our schools (Kelly and Cohn 1988).

Kelly's report establishes the pain and misery of being verbally abused and notes that some 13% more Asian than any other ethnic group of students in the survey reported being called names by other students. And the amount of physical violence experienced by Asian students in our schools leads *The Burnage Report* to conclude that:

This evidence suggests that for Asian students, girls no less than boys, schooling takes place in an atmosphere of constant intimidation. The attacks come apparently from nowhere, and the severity of the physical damage done to the individuals targeted seems to depend completely on luck. The extent of the psychological damage done to students concerned, as individuals and in terms of their collective identity, is no doubt immeasurable (*The Burnage Report*, p.258).

Ten months after the harassment project began at Lamont School, I conducted interviews with three students at the school. Up until then I had worked only with staff and I considered it important to learn the views of the students. The students were selected by the senior member of staff responsible for the project. All three had experienced bullying and harassment to a greater or lesser extent; two were white and one Asian. Their accounts appear in Chapter 4.

Each was asked the same questions, which formed the basis of discussion with me. I explained my role and the purpose of the interview and reassured them that I would not use their real names in my account of the interview. Two of the three appeared particularly to welcome the opportunity to discuss the issue of bullying and make their thoughts and feelings known.

The gender and race implications of bullying behaviour amongst girls

This study of a girls' single-sex school suggests that the degree and extent of bullying can be as widespread as in an all-boys school, though the nature of it varies considerably. Primarily, girls are 'bitchy' towards one another, though, as we have seen, it often does not stop at that. The range and level of physical violence can be as horrific and frightening as in an all-boys school. One of the girls involved in establishing the 'bully line' at another local all-girls school recalls being pushed onto the bonnet of an oncoming car, while Pratibha's bruises tell their own story.

Why do girls behave in this way? Strangely, it seems to be one way — and dare I say an almost acceptable way — of acquiring respect, power and status in the eyes of one's friends and classmates (even though popularity is not necessarily the result achieved). Being a bully becomes synonymous with being 'tough'.

Aggressive bullying behaviour can also serve, amongst such groups, as a direct challenge to and a way of resisting the accepted notions of femininity in

British society as the antithesis of being strong. At its worst, the traditional model of femininity is weak, needy and pathetic — not a model to which most young women today would aspire.

For some young women, seeking their feminine identity through the traditional route of boyfriends, make-up and being 'good' is simply not enough. They want these things and more besides. They seek to be equal to the male members of their families and their male friends and can match fist with fist. It would seem, moreover, in some instances, that if the academic route is perceived as an impossible means of acquiring power and status then power needs to be sought by another route — and one route may be bullying.

Some girls will maintain that they were simply 'having a bit of fun' and did not realise the hurt that they were causing. If they then stop bullying when the reality has been pointed out, they can be given the benefit of the doubt. Whatever the reason for the bullying, it is imperative that discussion with students about the issues takes place within the curriculum. Education is a very powerful tool in combating bullying and harassment and a commitment to the principles of 'equality and quality' means that tackling bullying must be part of the education delivered by the school.

Female victims do not have to be afraid, as male victims do, that they will be told to 'take it like a man' if they report that they are being bullied. Yet fear of reprisals and of being the centre of attention makes it equally daunting to tell. Many girls are also concerned lest they cause their already overburdened parents more bother. Pratibha, for instance had not kept her mother up to date with the latest occurrences because her mother was in hospital and she did not wish to worry her.

Friendships and disputes between friends have been found to be one of the main reasons for the bullying behaviour of girls and are the two most common features that distinguish the bullying behaviour of girls from that of boys. Excluding a friend from a friendship group is common amongst girls and may not be recognised as bullying by either teacher or the bullies and victims themselves. Besag (1989), in her analysis of the role of friendships in bullying amongst girls, concludes:

> Research on bullying suggests that boys seek power and dominance, whereas girls need a sense of affirmation and affiliation, a feeling of belonging and a shared intimacy expressed in exchanging confidences and gossip... This need for intimacy is manifest in bullying: bullies either exclude the targeted girl from the intimate group or, by use of malicious gossip, they try to prove that whereas they are acceptable, the discredited victim is not. This type of ploy can be executed with the skill of an army general on manoeuvres (p.41).

Teachers often see bullying by African-Caribbean girls as confirmation of their stereotype of this ethnic group as all 'loud, aggressive troublemakers' (Griffin, 1985, p.17) who are difficult for the school to handle. It is highly probable that such stereotyping has contributed significantly to the disproportionately high numbers of African-Caribbean students expelled from state schools (ILEA Research and Statistics 1196/88) and to their over-representation in EBD schools and the like. African-Caribbean students are aware of these views. Most wish to prove that they are wrong and will endeavour to do so but some do conform to the stereotype. We need to examine (as with all bullying behaviour) why this is so. We need also to examine the reality of being a young black woman in Britain in the '90s and to share this reality with our students — both black and white. The 'we treat them all the same' philosophy, which means that such differentiation is not openly acknowledged and discussed, can cause untold damage.

The bullying by African-Caribbean students of Asian students and in some instances between Caribbean and African students seems incomprehensible at first. 'After all, they're all black aren't they?' I often hear white teachers say. The naivety of this response must be replaced by a rational exploration of the underlying issues: for many African-Caribbean students, joining in with or leading the bullying of Asian students can be seen as one possible means of gaining acceptance by their white peers. Furthermore, such a liaison reduces the likelihood of being themselves on the receiving end of any racial bullying.

The girls of African-Caribbean descent who have little knowledge or understanding of their own historical past and cultural identity find the so-called 'strangeness' of Asian culture and African culture as unacceptable as do their white peers. Caribbean culture, which superficially seems similar to that of white, British culture (which is certainly not homogeneous) is seen as far more acceptable in this white society because there are fewer cultural differences. The historical devaluing of Caribbean creoles as 'broken English', nontheless suggests a clear language link with the majority ethnic community, whereas Asians and Africans speak many different languages. The greater the perceived difference, the greater the level of hostility:

> The hostility of white students tends to be general in nature and extends to diverse groups such as West Indians, Indians, Pakistanis, Jews and Cypriots as well as the handicapped groups such as the mentally ill and people with cerebral palsy (spastics) and epilepsy. However, a clear rank order of hostility can be distinguished and Jews and Pakistanis are the most rejected ethnic groups, while West Indians are less so, (Kelly and Cohn, 1988, p.44).

Finally, African-Caribbean students within the school subculture are often seen as the leaders in fashion, dance and sport (all valuable cultural capital in the school playground) and are, therefore, to be emulated rather than rejected and scorned.

Thus for many African-Caribbean students, lack of knowledge of their pre-colonial, pre-slavery history and a consequent lack of pride in their original African heritage serves to maintain the illusion of their similarity to white Britons and their distance from their Asian and African classmates. Until schools begin to address these gaps in the knowledge of their African-Caribbean students, inter-ethnic strife, involving black against black will continue to be a feature of multiracial schools.

Black supplementary schools have always played an important role in helping black children to reclaim their black identity, to value it and be proud of it. The state schooling system must also play its part. The untold damage caused by viewing education as simply a process which transmits white, middle class cultural values (Grace, 1987) must be addressed if equal opportunities regarding race, sex and class are to have any validity. This point is strongly made in the ILEA final report on equal opportunities (1990) and in *The Burnage Report* (1989) and its conclusions.

When bullying is of a racist nature, involving white against black, we again need to look to the wider society for its origins and to understand that schools will inevitably reflect, to a large extent, the practices and beliefs of that society. Hence pupils bring into school the racist attitudes and beliefs that permeate British society. These beliefs and attitudes cannot be dealt with by a simple act of suspension for a racist bullying offence. Without addressing the issue of racism and racial harassment within the school curriculum, the school is certain to be ineffective in its management of such offences and, as we have seen, often only makes a bad situation worse for an already distressed victim.

We need to look again at and question our understanding of multicultural antiracist education. For whose benefit is it? and what are we trying to achieve? are fundamental questions to be asked.

There follows a list of detailed recommendations for the school.

Recommendations for Lamont Girls' School

1.   The school must unambiguously declare its position with regard to racism, sexism, bullying and harassment, and do so in a manner that parents and students can understand. (*The Burnage Report*, 1989).

2.   The school needs to work towards creating an ethos which is truly antiracist and antisexist. This has implications for structural organisation; for example, for staffing, use of language and resources as well as for the curriculum.

3.   Given the extent of racial harassment identified by the school, a firm stance must be taken on:

   a.   dealing with racist abuse whenever it occurs;

   b.   dealing with the concept of racism within the curriculum, so providing possibilities for students to explore its origins, processes of transmission and the damaging consequences for both perpetrators and victims, and

   c.   teach a curriculum which is antisexist and antiracist and which challenges class oppression in both content and delivery.

   The awareness of staff on these issues must be addressed first of all. Staff will not feel confident or able to deal with these issues if they do not first have a chance to clarify their own views and ideas. As a starting point, the Inservice training programme concerning prejudice and racism that the present author and another facilitator presented to heads of year in summer 1989, needs to be cascaded to other members of staff.

4.   Strategies must be developed to create a climate in the school in which students feel able to report incidents in the knowledge that they will be listened to and swift action taken. Ongoing support needs to be provided to both victim and bully. (Follow-up work with the bully must take place if the bullying behaviour is not to be repeated. Yates and Smith found in their study (1989) that two thirds of those identified reported that no-one had talked to them about their bullying either at home or at school.

5.   The school needs to ensure that the disciplinary sanctions used do not cause further distress for the victim. Transferring the victim into another class for example, may make the bully feel she has won; whilst excluding her and then failing to follow up and monitoring her behaviour, when she returns to school, may lead her to believe that this is not a serious issue. Exclusion on its own is not enough.

6. The school now needs to create a climate in which incidents of bullying and harassment are reported, recorded and monitored. Such monitoring can help the school determine whether the strategies in use are being effective.

7. Harassment and bullying need to be constantly present on the agenda of staff meetings and heads of years and tutors meetings. Staff need to discuss regularly the nature of the bullying behaviour occurring in the school. As we have seen, girls frequently bully by means of exclusion and rejection, which staff often do not always recognise as bullying.

8. There needs to be regular discussion with and questionnaires to pupils about their perceptions of harassment and bullying in the school.

9. There needs to be a thorough review of staffs' classroom management strategies, as well as of the organisational structures of the school. For example: are teachers ignoring the polarisation of different ethnic groups evident in the seating arrangements in the classroom? If so, the teacher is actually reinforcing it and contributing to its continuation by refusing to acknowledge it. Are staff allowing racist remarks to go unchallenged because they fear the reprisals of white students or lack sympathy for the plight of the Asian students, taking the view that they 'deserve it', that they 'bring it upon themselves'?

10. All cultures — and that includes working class culture — are to be valued within the school and the curriculum. This is far too frequently taken for granted, allowing white students to claim that 'we are always having to learn about them' and demanding 'what about us?'

11. The school's newly drafted anti-harassment charter is to be discussed widely with the whole community: students, teaching staff, ancillary and support staff, parents and governors. The charter should be included in the school's handbook for parents and discussed with students and their parents/guardians during interviews with new intake and new arrivals.

12. The school council, as the voice of the student body, is to be more actively involved in monitoring the experiences of students with regard to bullying and harassment and in involving the whole school in debate about how to develop a collective response to these and other issues.

13. There needs to be regular inservice training for all staff around these issues so that there is a whole school response and consistency of approach.

School B — Bankside Boys' School

The questionnaire used in the summer term of 1990 with students in years seven and eight, to ascertain students' perceptions of bullying in the school ten months after the start of the harassment project, appeared in Chapter 5.

What the responses highlight is the extent of bullying of younger boys by older boys and the amount of physical violence which appears to pervade the school. Furthermore, physical violence is often linked to the extortion of money, so that the bully, in fact, doubly gains: a financial reward coupled with the subjugation of another individual.

Racial harassment was not dealt with specifically by the questionnaire so the extent of racial harassment in the school is less easily determined. However, we do know from the student interviews that it certainly takes place and that a single attack often incorporates verbal abuse, physical violence and, frequently, extortion of money.

I conducted interviews with three of the students from year eight who had completed the questionnaires on bullying earlier in the year and who had been involved in tutorial work concerning bullying. The questions were the same for Lamont School and I explored the students' answers during ensuing conversations.

The students were relatively young (age 12-13) so their understanding of the issues and their ability to articulate their thoughts and feelings was somewhat limited in comparison to the slightly older (14/15 year old) students from Lamont. As one saw in Chapter 5, however, one of the boys interviewed impressively and his level of awareness was outstanding.

The gender and race implications of bullying behaviour amongst boys

Besag (1989) concludes:

> There does seem to be a difference in the bullying behaviour of girls and boys — girls resort to physical aggression less often than boys, instead preferring social exclusion or malicious rumour (Roland, 1988).

Research into gender identity indicates that whilst biological factors may have a part to play, they are heavily outweighed by sociological and cultural determinants in defining our 'masculinity' or 'femininity'. The question, then, is: what part does masculinity play in determining the bullying behaviour of boys and what can be done to challenge this concept and its contribution to such destructive behaviour.

The dominant form of masculinity in Western culture embodies men's social power over women. It emphasises force, authority, aggressiveness (Connell et.al. 1987, p.19).

It is easy to see how bullying can be viewed as almost normal behaviour, in a society where the characteristics of 'force, authority, aggessiveness' are portrayed to its young men as highly desirable and proof of masculinity. Any deviation from the so-called norm is to be feared. Society perceives deviation as an ever-present threat; hence the scorn and ridicule heaped on gay men and those perceived as effeminate or weak because they cannot or will not live up to the dominant model. Witness the language of much verbal abuse in the playground amongst boys: terms like 'poof', 'poofter', 'queer', 'homo' are commonplace.

If force and authority cannot be achieved through the generally more acceptable routes of academic success or sporting achievement then bullying can be a creditable second best. Males in our society are socialised to believe that they are the holders and the wielders of power and the evidence proves that this is, in fact, the case. 'Men earn 90 per cent of the world's income and own 99 percent of its property,' the *New Internationalist* tells us. 'They also commit 90 percent of crimes of violence and 100 percent of rapes' (September, 1987 p.5). Every male in our society has to find his own way of claiming that power which, he has been socialised to believe, is his birthright. Physical violence is often viewed as a virtually acceptable means of claiming that power.

This then is the arena of masculinity in which bullying operates. Askew (1989) maintains that: 'Bullying is a major way in which boys are able to demonstrate their manliness' (p.65), and observes that 'even though a boy might be physically weaker than another, to be able to 'take it like a man' is usually considered to be a good second best masculine quality' (p.65). She concludes that: 'In this sense bullying can be seen as a manifestation of pressures put on boys to conform to male stereotypes' (p.65).

Many boys are actively encouraged by their parents to be proud of being aggressive and Dunning et.al. (1988) refer to 'families with a positive attitude to aggression.

Besag (1989) refers to several studies which show how parenting practice can be 'highly influential in controlling or encouraging aggressive behaviour' p.36). However, aggressive behaviour is not a feature to be attributed only to the working class, the disadvantaged or the poor. Highly stylised and ritualistic bullying behaviours have always had a part to play in the public school system (Walford 1989) and throughout the ranks of the British army: in fitting men to take their place in society.

We are proud of the Army, but we have to recognise that the power structure of the forces and the *type of training* (my emphasis) required to produce tough soldiers create soil for bullying '(Hansard 26 January 1988).

Boys' schools, in particular, would do well to take heed of this warning, for it suggests that they too, with their often competitive, authoritarian and aggressive ethos, can provide fertile breeding grounds for bullying behaviour. Lane (1989), whilst researching bullying at a boys' school, quotes a member of staff who claimed:

> 'This is a boys' school. You have to accept bullying. If a child can't take it they should be in another school' (p.95).

Given the construct of masculinity that exists in our society, is it so surprising that sexual harassment is such a common feature of all-boys schools? Bankside is no exception. Women staff in some boys' schools are often subjected to degrading and offensive remarks, and a continuum of violent, physical abuse ranging from pinches and grabs through to, in some cases, actual physical attack from males: both students and staff.

The majority of men, whatever their race or class, are reared to devalue women and to regard them as subordinate to men. Women are often perceived as a threat to their masculinity and must be kept in place through rape, other physical abuse, all the way to murder. More general is the practice of verbal abuse and a relegation of the female form to an 'object', whether of desire or scorn. Benn (*Spare Rib,* July 1985) posed the question 'Isn't sexual harassment really about masculinity?' and the answer would seem to be a resounding 'yes'. Huge changes are needed in the views promulgated in all-boys schools and mixed schools if we want them to become safer places for female colleagues and students.

Detailed recommendations follow.

Recommendations for Bankside Boys' School

Unlike the girls' school, Lamont, Bankside had not specifically identified any single aspect of bullying for particular attention. The four main areas perceived by the school as demanding immediate and equal attention were extortion, physical violence, verbal abuse and racial harassment. In the view of many of the boys, verbal abuse was common and a seemingly inevitable part of school life whereas physical violence posed the greatest threat. Both Sanjay and Joseph, who had been on the receiving end of physical violence, were small and totally unable to defend themselves physically against larger and more aggressive boys. The degree of fear in their daily lives was extremely high and very distressing.

Although the school strives to be orderly and well-disciplined (evident in its pastoral and disciplinary systems) there is obviously a sub-culture of violence and extortion that needs to be addressed. Many studies of primary school children about to transfer to secondary school reveal that their greatest fear about transfer is that they will be bullied. Taylor's study (1987) revealed that bullying caused parents more anguish than any other school problem.

1.   As part of its primary-secondary transfer programme, then, the school will need to look again at ways to minimise this fear for its new intake, so as to ensure that it does not become a reality for any student.

2.   The school needs to develop its own working definition of bullying. From my interviews with the students and staff it would appear that there are a significant number of one-off attacks which the school may well wish to define as bullying, even though many definitions of bullying specify that the attacks must be repeated over a period of time (for example, Besag 1989). But at this school, where attacks are often unprovoked, the victim powerless to defend himself and frightened by the experience, then it would seem that bullying has occurred. It is enough that the boys are fearful that it *may* happen again.

3.   The boys interviewed said that the school dealt with incidents of bullying in a satisfactory manner when they occurred. What is now needed is for a climate to be created in the school that allows bullying to be discussed as a whole-school issue, so the school can begin to be more proactive rather than merely reactive. Stephenson and Smith (1987/89) found that there were definite factors which caused some schools to have a much lower incidence of bullying than others:

> The teachers expressed articulate, considered and also purposeful views on bullying which emphasised the need for prevention where- as this was less apparent in the high bullying schools (O'Moore, 1989, p.6).

4.   The role of the bystander is an important one — it can indirectly contribute to bullying. By watching and not acting, one becomes indirectly involved. Developing an anti-bullying ethos must include teaching students to adopt strategies to avoid becoming complicit in the bullying acts they witness. Strategies might include taking action by informing an adult, and not tolerating bullies in the same social group (see Tattum and Herbert, 1990, p.30).

5.   Racial harassment featured in the accounts of all three boys — either from their own experience or in their accounts of bullying they had observed in

the school. Again, we need to look at white racism, and also at the factors contributing to bullying between different ethnic minority groups. The bullying of an Asian student by an African-Caribbean student crops up again, as at Lamont school. We can assume that factors similar to those relating to the bullying behaviour of some African-Caribbean girls, and already discussed, apply also to African-Caribbean boys. Lack of a real sense of cultural and ethnic identity and a copying of the attitudes of the dominant and oppressor group, to which one strives to belong, may explain — though it does not excuse — this behaviour.

6. Whilst swift action must be taken to deal with any form of bullying, it is important to stress that it is the bully's *behaviour* which is unacceptable and not the bully as a human being. Schools need to find ways to enable students to develop a strong and positive sense of self and of their historical past. The stereotyping of white working class boys as violent and aggressive and of African-Caribbean boys as aggressive trouble makers with above average sexual appetites (or even positive stereotypes: as sporting, musical and with a natural sense of rhythm and 'natural' talent) must be challenged. The full range of career possibilities must be seen as within their grasp if their potential is to be truly maximised.

7. Bullying between the members of different ethnic minority groups often serves to divert attention away from white racism and racial harassment. A teacher at a school in south London once asked me: 'Well, what's the difference? Black girls fight each other as well. Just the other day six black girls were suspended for fighting amongst themselves'. Such attitudes serve to obscure and so deny the horrendous specificities of white racism within British society with its chauvinism, inequalities of access to housing, education and employment and the categorisation of black people in Britain as immigrants and second class citizens. The fact that African-Caribbean students attack Asian students or vice versa does not challenge the principal imbalances of power within this society, whereas when whites attack Asians and other black ethnic minority groups, this serves to uphold and maintain that power.

8. Teacher attitudes will also have to be considered. Far too often, black boys become victims of self-fulfilling prophesies — no good is expected of them and this is exactly how things turn out. Lane's study, carried out over a number of years in several Islington schools, which tracked the development of behavioural problems of some one hundred pupils revealed that 'schools did make a difference' in helping either to reinforce or to challenge and help overcome the pattern of poor behaviour (Lane, 1989, p.98).

9. INSET concerning harassment and bullying is now required for all staff and students. To date, these issues have been addressed only in years seven and eight. Work done in the lower school will be swiftly undermined if staff and students in the upper school are not involved. Years nine to twelve must now be involved so that a whole-school approach can be developed.

10. The school needs to determine strategies for dealing with aggressive, violent behaviour. This will require an exploration of masculinity in society and the modelling for students of alternative value systems, based on negotiation, non-violent conflict resolution strategies and the re-channelling of aggression into assertion.

11. Given the amount of sexism identified in the school, which undoubtedly contributes to the high level of sexual harassment, the school will need to examine afresh the strategies currently used to deal with sexism. There needs to be close monitoring of the number of women on the staff, the positions they hold, their responsibilities and their ethnicity. The following questions also need to be asked:

- What support mechanisms exist for women who have been sexually harassed?

- How are incidents of sexual harassment dealt with? Are they monitored?

- Is the authority of women members of staff undermined by the fact that male colleagues in senior positions are always seen to do the disciplining and reprimanding?

- Do men on the staff indicate by their actions a 'do as I say, not as I do' philosophy? That is, is their behaviour towards their female colleagues beyond reproach or do they belittle women in subtle and not so subtle ways, such as by unnecessary touching, ogling women staff deemed physically attractive and verbally abusing those who are not?

- If sexual harassment incidents are monitored, what are the outcomes of this monitoring?

- How is sexism being addressed within the curriculum and within the organisational structures of the school?

- Do all staff challenge incidents of sexist behaviour by students?

This study constantly affirmed the positive role that the local education authority can play in supporting schools as they challenge bullying and harassment. Clear recommendations for the LEA emerged.

Recommendations for the LEA

1. The LEA should state unequivocally its position with regard to harassment and bullying, racism and sexism and restate its legal responsibility to provide a safe learning environment (Race Relations Act 1976, Section 71).

2. The LEA should declare its commitment to providing an education service which is antisexist and antiracist in practice. To this end, it needs to develop clear equal opportunities policies, with strategies for policy implementation, review and evaluation.

3. To assist schools, the LEA needs to develop clear policy, guidelines and strategies (for both students and staff) with regard to harassment and bullying, in consultation with schools, parents, local community groups and other service agencies (for example, social services, the neighbourhood offices, the police, the schools' psychological service, child guidance, youth centres). Harassment and bullying are of concern both locally and nationally, so demand both local and national responses.

4. Through its Inspectorate, support must be offered to institutions in the form of training for staff in both developing awareness of harassment and bullying and in how to create an ethos which reduces these behaviours to a minimum. Training needs to be directed at both whole school management and classroom management. Clear systems are needed for the review and evaluation of the new procedures put in place.

5. Clear systems for the reporting, recording and monitoring of incidents of bullying and harassment need to be established. Incidents of a racist or sexist nature should be monitored separately. It is vital that the LEA knows what is happening in its institutions in this regard, so as to assess requirements and offer support. An incident form should be drafted, to be used by all institutions, and all incidents monitored at least once each term by the LEA. A senior officer should be designated responsibility for ensuring that reporting, recording and monitoring are effectively carried out.

6. Exclusions for reasons of harassment and bullying need to be monitored.

7. The LEA's progress in addressing these issues needs to be regularly reported to education sub-committee.

8. A positive climate should be created whereby schools are able to meet together to discuss these issues regularly and to exchange information and good practice.

9.   There needs to be regular questioning of students, parents and staff regarding their perceptions of how these issues are being dealt with.

10.   The LEA needs to offer support to female students and staff experiencing sexual harassment in their institutions. A senior officer should be designated, to whom incidents can be reported in confidence and from whom advice and support can be sought.

11.   Similarly, the LEA should offer support to black and ethnic minority students and staff experiencing racial harassment in their institutions. A senior officer should be designated, to whom incidents can be reported in confidence and from whom advice and support can be sought.

12.   Guidance should be provided to schools on how to deal with incidents of harassment and bullying involving their students but which happen outside school.

Chapter 7
Wider implications of the research

This study has focused principally on the four areas identified in the introduction and this concluding chapter draws them together in the attempt to present an overview on developing a LEA approach and, consequently, a whole-school approach for dealing with harassment and bullying in single-sex schools.

a) The single-sex versus mixed school debate

Whilst single-sex girls schools are generally far 'safer' environments for girls in terms of avoiding sexual harassment from male students, girls-only schools can be just as unsafe for certain groups of girls in terms of behavioural problems and particularly bullying and harassment.

This study found that as high a percentage of the students at Lamont girls' school as at Bankside boys' school experienced bullying as either victim or bully. It seems that we need to look beyond the sex of the school population for an explanation of why this behaviour is so widespread in both institutions.

b) The school effectiveness debate and its contribution to developing a whole school approach

Most researchers now agree that some schools are much more effective than others in promoting good work and behaviour (The Elton Report, 1989).

That schools have an effect on their students' standard of behaviour as well as their academic performance is now accepted, indeed incontrovertible. Studies such as Rutter (1979), Smith and Tomlinson (1989), and Elton (1989), all demonstrate this to be so, and the body of research evidence continues to grow. Whilst race, sex and class dynamics obviously play a part in determining overall student performance, the schooling experience far outweighs these and other factors. Schools which have a low incidence of bullying do so not by chance but by a concerted effort on the part of the whole school to recognise the problem, to do something about it and to continue to do something about it (O'Moore, 1989).

The message to heads and teachers is clear. It is that they have the power, through their own efforts, to improve standards of work and behaviour and the life chances of their pupils (The Elton Report, 1989, p.88).

A simple statement of fact but one that is extremely important. Even at a time of huge cuts in spending on education, of low teacher morale, excessive workloads and physical and emotional stress, the reality remains that some schools are better able than others to provide a caring, supportive and yet stimulating and challenging learning environment for their students. In such institutions problems of poor behaviour are generally reduced to a minimum. How we manage our schools is crucial. The role of the head and the senior management team in setting the tone cannot be too heavily emphasised. On the one hand, this may seem a daunting task yet, on the other, it can be genuinely empowering for the head and the staff of a school. Elton concludes:

> Our visits to schools convinced us that, while good heads can have different personal styles, consistent themes run through effective school management. These include clear aims for teachers and pupils and good staff morale and team work. Effective leadership tends to produce a positive atmosphere and a general sense of security (The Elton Report, 1989, p.91).

c) ## Factors contributing to harassment and bullying in single sex schools

Bankside Boy's School

The competitive, aggressive and often 'macho' and sexist environment of all-boys schools undoubtedly contributes to the creation of a school culture in which aggression and violence are frequently celebrated, while gentleness and non-violence are treated with derision. An environment which advocates the 'survival of the fittest' creates a situation of 'every man for himself'. Only the toughest and the shrewdest survive. Changing such an ethos poses enormous challenges for staff and students in all-boys schools but challenge it we must, if all students are to be allowed to take an active part in their schooling and to be given the chance to succeed.

Such changes necessitate changes also in the attitudes and practices of male members of staff, who provide role models for the students in their charge. Collaborative learning techniques and classroom management and teaching strategies based on sharing, mutual support and an ethos that allows feelings to be explored and expressed in discussions, are part of the way forward. Disciplinary sanctions which depend on the threat of violence and/or ridicule must be replaced with sanctions that enable students to reflect upon and question their misbehaviour, knowing that it is their behaviour which is unacceptable and not they themselves (see recommendations for Bankside School).

Lamont Girls' School

Bullying amongst girls dispels the myth of girls and women as being exclusively caring, passive and non-aggressive — particularly when physical violence is involved. The young women perpetrating this type of behaviour, both in the school and in the local community (Packington Project Report, 1990), are possibly seeking status and a sense of worth in a society whose values and symbols of success seem to be out of their reach. Blaming the 'Asians' and 'Blacks' for taking, as they see it, their jobs and houses, means they need look no further to find a reason for the low status society has accorded them. The majority of students involved in racial harassment at Lamont School are working class (the school serves a predominantly white, working class catchment area) and some share the racist beliefs and attitudes of their families and friends. Schools must address these issues and provide forums where discussion around such issues can take place and where students can safely examine their beliefs and attitudes.

Being female — black or white — in Britain today is an issue for all students and staff. Young women need to explore the opportunities and options available to them and should be presented with as wide a range of options and role models as possible. They need also to be given the opportunity to achieve their full potential in the classroom. This means that schools must tackle race, sex and class oppression openly and with confidence, and provide situations which will allow the young women to develop their confidence and self-esteem and allow them to be assertive rather than passive or aggressive (see recommendations for Lamont Girls' School).

d) The LEA

Finally, but not least, the importance of the LEA in assisting institutions to address harassment and bullying needs to be stated again. As an officer of the LEA, this research study has provided me with knowledge which will be of tremendous help in the development of LEA policy, guidelines and strategies for supporting institutions and individuals to provide a learning environment free of harassment and bullying (see recommendations for the LEA).

References

Arnot, M. (1985) 'How shall we educate our sons?' in Deem, R. (Ed.) *Co-education Reconsidered.* Milton Keynes, The Open University Press

Askew, S. (1989) 'Aggressive Behaviour in Boys: To What Extent is it Institutionalised?' in Tattum, D. and Lane, D. (Eds.) *Bullying in Schools.* Stoke-on-Trent, Trentham Books

Besag, V. (1989) *Bullies and Victims in Schools,* Milton Keynes, Open University Press

Bourne, J. (1983) 'Towards an Antiracist Feminism'. *Race and Class,* 25, 1pp. 1-21.

Burgess, A. (1990) 'Co-education: the disadvantages for schoolgirls' in *Gender and Education,* Vol.2, No.1.

Chodorow, N. (1971) 'Being is doing: a cross-cultural examination of the socialisation of males and females in Deem, R. (Ed.) *Co-education Reconsidered,* Milton Keynes, The Open University Press.

City of Coventry Education Dept. (1989) *Gender Equality: From Analysis to Action,* Coventry.

Goleman, J. (1966) *Equality to Educational Opportunity,* Washington DC, United States Government Printing Office

Commission for Racial Equality (1987) *Living in Terror,* London, CRE

Commission for Racial Equality (1988) *Learning in Terror,* London, CRE

Committee of Enquiry Chaired by Lord Elton (1989) *Discipline in Schools,* London, HMSO

Connell, B. Radican, N. and Martin, P. (1987) 'The Evolving Man' *The New Internationalist,* 175, pp.18-20

Dunning, E. Murphy, P. and Williams, J. (1988) *The Roots of Football Holliganism: An Historical and Sociological Study,* London, Routledge and Kegan Paul

Elliott, M. (1986) *Kidscape Project,* unpublished research. The Kidscape Primary Kit, Kidscape, 82 Brock St, London, W1Y 1YP

Forward, D. (1989) 'A Guide to Action Research' in Lomax, P. (Ed.) *The Management of Change,* Avon, Short Run Press Ltd.

Goldstein, A. Apter, S. and Harootunian, B. (1984) *School Violence.* New Jersey, Prentice-Hall Inc.

Grace, G. (1987) 'Teachers and the State in Britain: A Changing Relation' in Lawn, M. and Grace, G. (Eds.) *Teachers and the Culture and Politics of Work. Lewes, Falmer Press*

Griffin, C. (1985) *Typical Girls? Young Women From School to the Job Market.* London, Routledge and Kegan Paul

Hooks, B. (1982) *Ain't I a Woman?* London, Pluto Press

Howe, R. (1974) 'The Education of Women' also 'Equal Opportunities for Women' in Stacey, J. et.al. (Eds.) *And Jill Came Tumbling After: Sexism in American Education.* New York, Dell.

Inner London Education Authority (1985) *The English Curriculum: Gender, ILEA English Centre.*

Inner London Education Authority (1985) *A Policy for Equality: Sex,* ILEA

Inner London Education Authority (1986) *Primary Matters: Some Approaches to Equal Opportunities in Primary Schools,* ILEA

Inner London Education Authority (1986) *Secondary Issues? Some Approaches to Equal Opportunities in Secondary Schools,* ILEA.

Inner London Education Authority (1986) *Suspensions and Expulsions from Schools — 1986/87,* RS 1196/88

Inner London Education Authority (1990) *Equal Opportunities Policy in ILEA: The Final Review of Initiatives and Implementation,* ILEA

Inter-Departmental Racial Attacks Group (1989) *The Response to Racial Attacks and Harassment: Guidelines for the Statutory Agencies.* London

Jones, C. (1985) 'Sexual Tyranny: Male Violence in a Mixed Secondary School' in Weiner, G. (Ed.) *Just a Bunch of Girls.* Milton Keynes, The Open University Press

Keise, C. (1989) *Harassment and Bullying: Developing a Whole School Approach,* unpublished article

Kelly, E. and Cohn, T. (1988) *Racism in Schools — New Research Evidence.* Stoke-on-Trent, Trentham Books

Lane, D. (1989) 'Violent Histories: Bullies and Criminality' in Tattum, D. and Lane, D. (Eds.) *Bullying in Schools.* Stoke-on-Trent, Trentham Books

Lees, S. (1987) 'The Structure of Sexual Relations in Schools' in Arnot, M. and Weiner, G. (Eds.) *Gender and the Politics of Schooling.* London, Hutchinson

Lowenstein, L. (1976) Perception and Accuracy of Perception of the Bullying Child of Potential Victims, unpublished research.

Mahoney, P. (1983) 'How Alice's chin really came to be pressed against her foot: sexist processes of interaction in mixed-sex classrooms' in *Women's Studies International Forum,* Vol.6, No.1, pp.107-115

Mahoney, P. (1985) *Schools for the Boys.* London, Hutchinson

Millman, V. (1987) 'Teacher as researcher: a new tradition for research on gender' in Weiner G. and Arnot, M. (Eds.) *Gender Under Scrutiny, New Inquiries in Education.* London, Hutchinson

Mitchell, A. (1984) *On the Beach at Canterbury,* London, Allison & Busby

Olweus, D. (1978) *Aggression in the Schools: Bullies and Whipping Boys.* Washington DC, Halstead Press

O'Moore, A. (1989) 'Bullying in Britain and Ireland: An Overview' in Roland, E. and Munthe, E. (Eds.) *Bullying: An International Perspective,* London, Fulton Publishers

Open University (1989) *Reluctant Masters. Can't we find a better word?* London, ILEA Reprographics Service

Packington Annual Report (1990) unpublished

Payne, I. (1980 2nd ed.) ' A Working Class Girl in Grammar School' in Spender, D. and Sarah, E. (Eds.) *Learning to Lose. Sexism and Education,* London, Women's Press

Pence, E. (1982) 'Racism — A White Issue' in Hull, T. Scott, P. and Smith, b. (Eds.) *All the Women are White, all the Men are Black but Some of Us are Brave,* New York, The Feminist Press

Phoenix, A. (1987) 'Theories of Gender and Black Families' in Weiner, G. and Arnot, M. (Eds.) *Gender Under Scrutiny: New Enquiries in Education,* London, Hutchinson

Report to the Department of Education and Science (1985) *Education for All,* London, HMSO, (The Swann Report)

Report of the Macdonald Inquiry into Racism and Racial Violence in Manchester Schools (1989) *Murder in the Playground: The Burnage Report,* London, Longsight Press

Reynolds, D. (1976) 'The Delinquent School' in Woods, P. (Ed.) *The Process of Schooling,* London, Routledge and Kegan Paul

Reynolds, D. and Reid, K. (1988) 'The second stage: towards a reconceptualisation of theory and methodology in school effectiveness research' in Westoby, A. (Ed.) *Culture and Power in Educational Organisations,* Milton Keynes, The Open University Press.

Rutter, M. et.al. (1979) *Fifteen Thousand Hours,* London, Open Books

Sarah, E. and Scott, M. and Spender, D. (1980- 2nd Edn.) 'The Education of Feminists: The Case for Single Sex Schools' in Spender, D. and Sarah, E. (Eds.) *Learning to Lose, Sexism and Education,* London, Women's Press

Sharpe, S. (1976) 'Just Like a Girl' in Spender, D. and Sarah, E. (Eds.) *Learning to Lose: Sexism and Education.* London, Women's Press

Smith, D. and Tomlinson, S. (1989) *The School Effect: a Study of Multicultural Comprehensives.* London, Policy Studies Institute

Spender, D. (1982) *Invisible Women the Schooling Scandal.* London, Writers and Readers Co-operative

Stanworth, M. (1981) *Gender and Schooling: a study of sexual divisions in the classroom.* London, Hutchinson

Stephenson, P. and Smith, D. (1989) 'Bullying in the Junior School' in Tattum, D. and Lane, D. (op.cit.)

Tattum, D. (1989) 'Violence and Aggression in Schools' in Tattum, D. and Lane, D. (op.cit.)

Tattum, D. and Herbert, G. (1990) *Bullying: a Positive Response.* Cardiff, SGIHE

Taylor, G. 'Bullying — 'Misery for the Child — Heartache for parents' *Mother Magazine,* June 1987

Walford, G. (1989) 'Bullying in the Public Schools: Myth and Reality' in Tattum, D. and Lane D. (op.cit.)

Walkerdine, V. (1989) *Counting Girls Out.* London, Virago

Wright, C. (1987) The relations between teachers and Afro- Caribbean pupils: observing multiracial classrooms' in Weiner, G. and Arnot, M. (Eds.) *Gender Under Scrutiny: New Inquiries in Education.* London, Hutchinson

Yates, C. and Smith, P. (1989) 'Bullying in Two English Comprehensive Schools' in Roland, E. and Munthe, E. (Eds.) *Bullying: An International Perspective.* London, Fulton.